A Guidebook for Cooperative Learning

A Technique for Creating More Effective Schools

Second Edition

**Dee Dishon
Pat Wilson O'Leary**

L𝐏 LEARNING PUBLICATIONS, INC.
Holmes Beach, Florida

ISBN 1-55691-111-4

Learning Publications, Inc.
5351 Gulf Drive
P.O. Box 1338
Holmes Beach, FL 34218-1338

Cover design: Barbara J. Wirtz

Printing: 6 5 4   Year: 8 7 6 5

Printed in the United States of America.

CONTENTS

Acknowledgments

This is a completely revised edition of our original guidebook (1984). Our first edition was viewed by some as practical tips for implementing David Johnson's and Roger Johnson's model of cooperative learning. This guidebook represents the changes we have made and the creation of a separate framework, the Dishon/Wilson O'Leary Model of cooperative learning.

We wish to thank all of those who have been our teachers over the years: David Johnson and Roger Johnson, from whom we first learned about cooperative learning; Liana Graves and Ted Graves who encouraged and supported us and our work through the International Association for the Study of Cooperation in Education (IASCE); and the teachers who taught us about cooperative groups by inviting us into their classrooms.

Thanks also go to our immediate families, Don Andress and Art and Artie O'Leary, who support us in our work and travel. We appreciate their continued encouragement.

*We dedicate this book to all who believe and work
as we do for cooperation on earth.*

FOREWORD

What could be more gratifying than seeing a complex subject illumined by an informed perspective that guides the examination of an abundance of details? Like the sun at midday or the full moon at night, this book does not hide complications or difficulties yet sheds light on the whole. Dee and Pat encourage us to believe we can each achieve the vision they share with us of a cooperative, effectively functioning classroom. We believe them because we are given principles to guide us to consciously chosen goals. We are assisted to examine our beliefs and behavior in a way that does not dampen our self esteem. Moreover, we know we will be coached and informed every step of the way.

We also discover we will not be forced to attempt attaining the entire picture before we have grasped the fundamentals. With infinite patience and compassion, our guides teach us how to total up small successes along the way, to learn in stages, and to be understanding of ourselves in each stage, not biting off more than we can thoroughly chew and digest. Starting with simple cooperative learning strategies and basic principles of designing a cooperative classroom, they take us to three-step and then five-step lesson planning, giving plenty of examples and anticipating every possible hitch. We are invited to see things exactly as they are, not simply because the authors wish to destroy rosy dreams of students who adore cooperating or instructional methods that provide a magic panacea, but in order to help us make realistic assessments of how to proceed, to overcome possible roadblocks, and to continue our journey along the unfolding path of cooperative education undeterred.

Time and again as I read, I wished to thank Pat and Dee for their honesty and authenticity. Clearly they have been in the tight spots they describe, and readers will not feel alone in their dilemmas. At the same time, I was grateful for their unfailing optimism which turned every possible "failure" into an opportunity for revelation and growth, every "mistake" from a wall into a door opening to new possibilities.

First steps in anything new can feel awkward and wobbly, but with Dee and Pat's Guidebook, plus access to the other resources they recommend, we know we will be supported and encouraged. And for those of us who have been using cooperative learning for some time, there are some surprises and some new lenses to focus on our favorite subject. The authors challenge each of us -- practitioners, developers, and researchers alike — to question the ways we have been thinking about or implementing our cooperative group work. Having brought together the best, the fullest of cooperative learning approaches, they expect of us the dedication, thoughtfulness, perseverance, and patience they model for us.

Their first and major offering is **clarity!** Reading this edition, I had a similar experience to when I devoured the first edition of the Guidebook. Once again, although I and cooperative learning as a field of endeavor are both further along the path, I am led to examine both my theory and my practice. I realize the vagueness of some of my concepts, the slip-shoddiness of some of my techniques. Yet every discovery is a gift, never a rebuke or a lecture. Pat and Dee are not only true professionals who never lose sight of the goal of better learning situations for ourselves and our students. They are also compassionate colleagues who recognize and have experienced the struggles of growing into egalitarian, fully collaborative learning communities, and they remind us to be kind to ourselves along the way.

Their second and equally welcome gift is **abundance.** Dee and Pat have learned in interaction with the international cooperative learning community, acknowledge its controversies and dialogues, and summarize these succinctly. They then make clear choices for the model they wish to present. Nor are they ideologues. Each choice is backed up with philosophical, empirical or pragmatic reasons, illustrated with the consequences of various alternatives they have observed in classrooms visited.

They have also learned from the teachers they have worked with over time and space. Pat and Dee credit these teachers for ideas they have incorporated in their workshops and book, and teachers' experiences and concerns have caused them to reconsider and change some of the recommendations made in this edition of the Guidebook. The authors' true grasp of collaborative principles have made this edition richer and more grounded in both knowledge and experience than the last. Vignettes from real classrooms bring cooperative learning to life. We are treated to an abundance of strategies and methods for each type of group work, of types of appropriate skills and tasks, of alternative room arrangements and techniques for forming different types of cooperative groups. But this is not a "help-yourself" smorgasbord of approaches. Pat and Dee are selective, both showing us why they have chosen certain offerings over others and giving us issues to consider when we make our own decisions and choices.

Perhaps best of all, this abundance of skills and techniques is fully matched and complemented with an equal abundance of heart. The thoughtfulness of these two excellent teachers and facilitators comes across to the reader as caring for both practitioners and their students. In this particular model of group work, we find a clear vision of what it take to produce truly cooperative learning at its zenith.

Liana Nan Graves, Cooperation in Creative Change
Editor, *Cooperative Learning* magazine publication sponsored by the
International Association for the Study of Cooperation in Education

COOPERATIVE LEARNING: THE VISION

A major effort in education today is to create effective schools through implementation of a *cooperative learning model*. Educators who seek a research-based model desire an effective method of instruction for teaching academics and social skills, as well as democratic values.

The specific steps outlined in this guide are grounded in educational research. They are based upon evidence which indicates that, under most conditions, instruction is more effective when students work in cooperative learning groups rather than in situations where competition and individualistic learning are emphasized.

The Dishon/Wilson O'Leary model of cooperative learning, as presented here, is a systematic model for helping educators teach the skills necessary for effective group work. Our goals for teachers are to help them:

- ◆ Recognize the value of group work as a process to learn social and academic skills and concepts, not just as another way to produce a product.

- ◆ Change their thinking about group work and learning: what it is and isn't; where it fits; how to use it.

- ◆ Observe student behavior and base decisions about group work on what they see and hear.

- ◆ Feel more positive and encouraged about social skills students feel safe to practice and exhibit in the classroom.

- ◆ Enjoy teaching more.

CHAPTER 1

Teachers can learn to support students as they:

* Make decisions about working together and solving problems.

* Learn subject matter and skills for thinking.

* Build positive relationships within groups and the classroom.

* Solve group problems with minimal teacher assistance.

* Enjoy the process of working together.

Cooperative learning procedures in our model are appropriate for all levels and content areas — from pre-school through graduate school. These procedures help students practice skills and explore concepts which are a part of the curriculum for their grade and subject area.

Students who work in cooperative groups learn important social skills which facilitate cooperation. With these skills, students relate appropriately to others who are different from them in terms of social background, race, gender, physical condition, intellectual skill, or social proficiency. Research shows that the consistent use of cooperative teaching methods in the classroom helps students learn and care about others. Students learn to not only tolerate individual differences, but to value them as well, which is of particular importance with our nation's increasing ethnic, religious, and lifestyle diversity.

In cooperative learning situations, students work and learn in groups. Of course, students working in groups is not new. Teachers have been using group methods for as long as there have been classrooms. None the less, many teachers tend to de-emphasize the use of groups because they have experienced group work in school settings to be disruptive and unproductive. This has resulted in their disillusionment with special group approaches to instruction. Furthermore, while most teachers recognize the value of cooperation and the benefits of students learning from each other, many allow their past frustrations to decrease their willingness to plan cooperative learning experiences.

We believe this guidebook has something to offer all teachers:

* For teachers who assert that they have been using cooperative learning for years (when in fact some of these teachers simply

push the desks together), we issue an invitation to stay open to new ways of thinking about learning and group work.

◆ For teachers who say they have tried cooperative learning and it just doesn't work because students don't like it, or it is too disruptive, or they just "can't cover the curriculum," we request an openness to other possibilities than the ones that haven't worked so far.

◆ For teachers who have had no formal training in cooperative learning and are creating marvelous learning experiences for their students, we offer a structure and some ideas that may strengthen their current group activities.

◆ For teachers who are well trained and currently implement some model of cooperative learning, we offer a variety of options they could choose from to support their present programs.

Some teachers mistakenly believe that particular personalities in their classrooms totally determine the outcome of special group work, regardless of how they organize group work. Of course, what the teacher does and does not do is critical to what students learn. There is nothing mystical about what enables teachers to successfully foster cooperative learning. We believe that the teacher's success depends upon the use of specific skills which can be taught and learned. There are skills which a teacher needs to know and skills which students must learn in order to work cooperatively with their peers. Without these student and teacher skills, group work will not be consistently successful and will require excessive teacher supervision.

How do you as a teacher acquire the skills needed for implementing cooperative learning? Knowledge and practice are needed. Knowledge of the required skills and how to teach these skills to students, combined with practice, will enable you to become proficient in facilitating cooperative learning experiences. This guidebook, implemented with your enthusiasm, determination, and humor, will help you acquire the necessary knowledge and structure for practicing this model of cooperative learning. You will then be able to teach students or adults to work productively and enjoyably in groups while achieving both academic and social goals.

Our efforts in writing and revising this guidebook are directed at reducing the energy expended on implementation of cooperative groups in the classroom. Our experience has taught us that all the research in the world or edicts from central office will not convince classroom teachers to try new techniques if they feel out of control of management details in the classroom. We offer specific ways to help you as a teacher be in control of the classroom during group work and feel successful.

There are numerous models of cooperative learning available to school districts, many of which are grounded in educational research. The quest seems to focus on how quickly a district can train teachers to use cooperative learning in every classroom in every school. We are concerned that educators are only looking at these short term goals rather than the long term goals of creating cooperative people within cooperative schools, communities, states, nations, the world. Since we know that institutionalizing any innovation takes years and only happens successfully if the innovation is mutually agreed upon and every effort is made to include educators, parents, and students in the process, cooperative learning seems like the perfect innovation to implement cooperatively!

Our hope for the planet is that our society's institutions and the people who are involved in them will show by example how to create cooperation on earth. Through that cooperation we can all be successful, happy, prepared to take on life's challenges, and be part of a community beyond ourselves, our friends and family. We believe that by including students in the learning process through the use of cooperative groups, we will create a citizenry that will learn to work through problems by consensus and face challenges through inclusion of all points of view.

COOPERATIVE LEARNING
IN ACTION

Cooperative groups are different from typical classroom groups in several significant ways. These differences are illustrated through a visit to a fifth grade classroom where successful cooperative learning experiences occur. There are five important principles which underlie successful cooperative learning experiences. They are: The Principle of Distributed Leadership; The Principle of Heterogeneous Grouping; The Principle of Positive Interdependence and Individual Accountability; The Principle of Social Skill Acquisition; and The Principle of Group Autonomy. The five principles are outlined, illustrated and then followed by a discussion of how to put them into effect. You will then have an opportunity to examine how your beliefs and behaviors match those necessary for successful implementation of this model of cooperative learning.

MR. JORDAN'S CLASS: AN ILLUSTRATION

As Walter Jordan's 32 fifth graders settle down after lunch, he asks for attention and announces that today's lesson on using reference materials to do research will be done in cooperative groups. Several students quickly ask, "Will we be in our Social Studies groups today, Mr. Jordan?"

"No, we will be getting into new groups because this unit will last for 2 weeks and it seems like a good time for you to work with some new people. We'll number off for new groups after I give some of the directions," he explains. "Your new group members will all find one another after I point to where you are to meet. Then I want each person to discuss the following topic."

Mr. Jordan writes the topic on the board: *One of my favorite places is _____ because_____*. "Each person is to have a chance to talk about this subject in the 3 minutes you have. Who can remind us why it's important to do a teambuilding topic before we start our group work? Jenarro, you look like you might remember."

"We need to get to know the people in our group. It's important that we do something first that isn't just the group job."

"Yes, thanks for giving us the benefit of your memory, Jenarro. Now, what do you need to remember before someone starts talking about the topic?"

"We need to give everyone wait time," responds Sheila.

"Right, Sheila. Who can remind us about wait time?"

"It's time to think and choose the answer you want to tell, 'cause you can only tell one. That's the rule."

"Thanks, Mario. And who remembers what groupmates do when someone is taking his or her turn?" Mr. Jordan nods at Bernard.

"We're supposed to show we're listening by not interrupting or asking questions, right?"

"Yes, that's what we all agreed to when we started group work. Who remembers and can tell Lien who hasn't been with us long, how we are seated during group time?"

"I can," says Teresa. "We always sit EEKK, eye to eye and knee to knee."

"And why do we sit so close?" inquires the teacher.

"If we don't it's hard to see and hear," remarks Ramona.

"That's for sure. So, class, what are you going to be doing during this 3 minutes?"

Several students join in to repeat directions, with Mr. Jordan nodding and smiling agreement. "It's time now to get into groups, so what numbers do you count off by if we want groups of 3 and our class size is 35?" The students become silent and thoughtful, apparently considering the question. They know this is not the time to respond, only think. This is one of the routines they have learned.

"OK, class. Turn to your neighbor and say what you think the answer is and why." A buzz begins as students turn to a person near them and begin talking quietly. Everyone has quickly turned so it seems that this, too, is part of classroom routine, as no one is left out for even a moment.

After a few seconds, Mr. Jordan raises his hand and stands quietly while students who see him begin raising their hands. The noise abates as more students finish speaking and raise their hands. "Thank you. Now, did your neighbor say a number over 10?" Hands go up. "Did your neighbor say a number over 12?" Some hands go down. "Who thinks their neighbor had the right answer? Jamal?"

"My neighbor thinks it is 11 because there are eleven 3's in 35."

"Well, then, what about the 2 left over? What does your neighbor think about that?"

"She says that makes 2 groups of 4. And I agree with her!"

"Well, did anyone else's neighbor have 11?" Most of the hands go up. "Looks like a lot of people were thinking clearly because it IS 11.

"Let's review what everyone does when you know who's in your group. Takesha, your hand is up."

"We act as if we're glad because it can hurt people's feelings if you act like you're sad or mad that they're in your group."

"Thank you. And what else do you keep in mind when finding out who's in your group? Yes, Jason?"

"Remember it's only a working relationship. You don't have to be friends to get along and work together."

"Yes, I agree. So it seems like time to count off. You agreed that you would be counting off by what number?"

"Eleven!" students reply.

"All right, Barry, why don't you start us off with #1."

When everyone has a number, Mr. Jordan points out where the groups are to meet. He informs them that they will have four minutes to accomplish this part of the task and sets the timer. The groups quickly form. Students each get a nearby chair which they pull up to one desk used as the shared writing surface. Students arrange themselves, and gradually each group has someone talking about a favorite place. Mr. Jordan walks between groups all the way around the room, interrupting no one, being sure there is room between groups so that he can move around. He then goes to the front of the room and puts a transparency on the overhead. When the timer goes off, students gradually raise hands until all talking has ceased and they turn so they can see Mr. Jordan.

"Who can tell us what one of your new groupmates said about a favorite place?" Several students share as the others listen. Mr. Jordan nods and smiles at each response.

"I want you all to think about what just happened in your group. How did you make sure that everyone got a turn? What did people do that insured that everyone got a chance to speak on the topic?"

Again, students are silent as they each sit, reflecting on the question. A discussion ensues with responses like "We each talked really fast;" "Sam started and then we just went around;" "Jaya asked who wanted to start."

"If your group included everyone that time, be sure to keep doing what you are doing. If you didn't, think about what you can do in this next time period to give everyone a turn. Now, here are the directions for what you're going to do next."

Most students turn completely around so they can see the directions which are revealed one at a time on the screen. Mr. Jordan reads them aloud.

Your group will receive one paper with states listed from one section of the United States.

Each person in your group will have a different source of information (atlas, World Almanac, geography textbook).

Your group is to reach consensus on each of the answers, using as many of the resources as possible. (You will list the resource and where the information was found on the group paper.)

Everyone in the group must be ready to be reporter. After group work one groupmate will be chosen randomly to give the group answers.

Each person is to be a writer. Write an answer someone else found, not your own.

Get as far as you can in this time period. Be sure to: check accuracy and include everyone's ideas and resource.

Each person will have to sign the paper at the end of work time to show agreement and participation.

Teacher's Role — Group questions only

Time limit: 15 min.
Start: _____ Stop: _____

"All resources, materials, your group paper and pencil are in the Materials Center. Only the Messenger may leave the group to get them. Please select someone who hasn't been a Messenger lately. At the end of work time, I will call several names from the Winner's Hat to report on one of their group's answers." Here Mr. Jordan holds up a blue plastic batting helmet that has slips of paper with names on them.

"You don't know which groups or which groupmates will be chosen, or which questions he or she will have to tell about, so be sure everyone is ready to respond."

"Do we get a grade on this, Mr. Jordan?" inquires Latosha.

"Each person will get a checkmark in the grade book if your group's paper is at least 80% correct. If it is not, your group will have a paper to repair until it is at least 80% correct. Also, you will need this information to help you in being successful on the next part of your group report."

"What about a social skill? Are we going to practice one today?" asks Hao. In response, Mr. Jordan reveals a sheet of paper taped to the board that is labeled "Respond to Ideas Respectfully" and which is divided into 2 columns titled "Looks Like" and "Sounds Like."

"As you know, we have practiced lots of social skills since the beginning of the year." Here Mr. Jordan moves his arm toward the far wall on which are displayed several large pieces of chart paper, each on a different social skill. The one we're practicing today is new in some ways and like others we have done in some ways. First, in a moment I want you to turn to your neighbor and tell your neighbor why you think I am giving you *this* social skill for this assignment. Now, think." There is a silence extending for several seconds. "Now, turn to your neighbor. Give your response and listen to your neighbor's answer. Remember that I will call on several people to tell me what their neighbor said."

Students turn toward a person close to them, exchange answers eagerly and then respond to the quiet signal. "Who is willing to tell us what your neighbor said? Yes, Jennifer?"

"My neighbor said that we may disagree about answers today and we don't want to get into arguments."

"Yes, that's true," replies Mr. Jordan. "And why might we forget to respond respectfully when we have differences of opinion?" Joshua raises his hand.

"Because we might just want to argue and we don't listen to each other."

"OK. Thank you. Who else will tell us what your neighbor said. Jamie?"

"My neighbor told me that being nice to people is a good thing to do because if you're not then some people don't want to help out in the group."

"So you wouldn't want that to happen in a group. Correct, Jamie?"

Jamie nods and smiles. Mr. Jordan continues, "Who can tell us why is it necessary to talk about disagreements?"

"We don't want to go along with an answer unless we're sure it's right or makes sense."

"Yes, Ann, and discussion and perhaps disagreement is the only way to be sure that *everyone* agrees and is convinced the answer is accurate."

"OK, so how would I know when I'm walking around during work time that people in your group are responding to ideas respectfully? What would it sound like?"

" 'I don't agree.' "
" 'Are you sure of that?' "
" 'That doesn't sound right to me.' "
" 'Good idea!' "
" 'I hadn't thought of that.' "

Mr. Jordan records the students' words with a smile and a nod for each. "What can 'Respond to Ideas Respectfully' look like?" His students give a variety of answers:

"Eye contact."
"Lean in."
"Smile."
"No frowny faces."

"What would that look like, Wayne?"
Wayne looks up with a straight face; no smile, no frown.

"Yes, I think that might work," says Mr. Jordan as he writes that up. "All right, I think you have the idea, class. Today while you are working, I will observe each group. I will use an observation form to record everything I see or hear that seems to me like responding to ideas respectfully. As you remember, I won't be observing your group for the whole time, but I want each of you to practice even when I'm not there. If you forget, remember the social skill when you see me near your group and think to yourself if you are responding to ideas respectfully."

If you have any questions during work time, what are you to do? Yes, Eric?"

"We have to ask everyone in our group and then if we still need help, we raise our hands and say that we have a group question."

"OK and then who asks me the question?"

"You call on anyone in the group you want to because everyone in the group should know the question if it's really a group question."

"Yes, you've got it. And will I interrupt your group or stop and talk to you as I go by? Yes, Darla?"

"No, Mr. Jordan, because you're invisible unless we ask a group question or you tell us you're interrupting."

"Right! Now, I would like you to think: what is the first thing you need to decide in your group?" He continues to check for understanding of directions by turning off the light in the overhead, then reminds students to pull tightly into their groups. As they begin work, he writes the start and stop time on the transparency.

As messengers begin leaving their groups to get materials, Mr. Jordan deliberately stays away from the Materials Center and begins filling in observation forms with names of students. He walks around, recording examples of the social skill which he can hear being used as students disagree about who is supposed to do what. Instead of reminding them of directions, though, he continues moving around the room, noting social skills as well as how resources are being used: which materials are being referred to most often, which scarcely at all.

After a few minutes of work time, one group appears to be having trouble. Sherry's chair is pushed away from the group; her arms are folded and her face is stern. The teacher looks over at the group but makes no move towards them until the other three students raise their hands. Mr. Jordan promptly approaches them.

"Is this a group question? Dana, what is the question?"

"Mr. Jordan, Sherry won't use the almanac that she's supposed to use to help us look up information. She says she doesn't care if we get the answers or not," Dana explains.

"Well, your group certainly has a problem. What have you done so far to encourage Sherry to participate?"

The group members glance at each other and back at their teacher. "We told her she'd better do it or we would tell you," Jason offers.

"I would like you to figure out three more ways to help invite Sherry to join the group. I'll be back in two minutes to see what your group has to report."

Walter Jordan then moves slowly around the room, continuing to mark the observation forms. He returns to Sherry's group after two minutes with a question. "What does your group have to report, Maria?"

"We decided that we can ask her to leave; we can ask her what she would like to do; we can offer to help her use the almanac," Maria reports. Sherry has unfolded her arms and appears to be following the conversation.

"You may not ask her to leave since she is a member of your group. You may use one of the other suggestions. Sherry, please move closer to the group and listen to the suggestions. I want you to work this out together. I'll be back soon to see what you have decided."

The teacher walks away and doesn't look over at the group again until he returns a short time later. "What has your group decided?"

"We asked her what she would like to do and she said we could help her use the almanac," reports Jason.

"Does that work for you, Sherry?" Sherry nods. "All right, let's see how your solution works."

When the timer sounds and students get quiet and turn to the front of the room, Mr. Jordan is smiling. "I am very impressed with how hard you have been working and how you are responding respectfully to one another. Let's start processing. If you have the group paper, please hold it up." A pause ensues until a sheet of paper is held up in each group. "Now pass the paper to the person to your right. This is the writer."

Mr. Jordan reveals the following statement on the overhead.

"Our group did well on *responding to others respectfully* by _____, _____, and _____ (three specific behaviors)."

"As you remember, you are to discuss what three behaviors could go in the blanks. All of you must agree before the writer copies down your answers. You have 2 minutes for this. Go!"

Mr. Jordan walks slowly around the room listening in on groups but not commenting. When the timer goes off, he says, "Writer, please be ready to tell us one of your behaviors that the group decided on. I will write it on the chart paper if it isn't already up. If someone in another group gives me the one you were going to say, choose another one when it is your turn."

As each reporter tells a behavior, Mr. Jordan writes up the new ones and puts a checkmark by those that are already up.

"In a moment, I will be returning your observation form. Huddle around it quickly and be ready to give me one behavior that isn't on our chart yet."

When Mr. Jordan has passed out all observation forms and students have taken a few seconds to look them over, he signals for quiet and hears several other behaviors that haven't been mentioned yet and writes them on the chart.

Sounds Like:	"What I think you mean is..."
	"I don't understand where you got that."
	Use names
Looks Like:	Eyebrows raised
	Pulled in close

"OK, we will keep this chart up to remind us all to respond to ideas respectfully at *all* times, not just during group work.

"Now let's hear some responses about your section of the United States. Take a minute to be sure that everyone in your group is ready to tell about any of the answers on the group paper."

The groups buzz as questions are asked and everyone prepares to be reporter.

"OK, let's see who our winners are." Mr. Jordan reaches into the baseball helmet and pulls out a name. "Barbara!" Everyone cheers and applauds for Barbara as she claps her hands and appears to be happy that she was chosen.

"Barbara, your group had the mid-Atlantic states. Show us their location on the map up front and tell us one fact you learned about them from the atlas."

Barbara and her group stand and move to the front of the room. She points out where the mid-Atlantic states are with no help from her group. "We discovered that all the mid-Atlantic states border the Atlantic Ocean." Applause greets her responses as the class appreciates her group's work.

Mr. Jordan pulls out three more names and the winners picked act as the group reporters, giving answers requested.

"Now, class, be sure that everyone in your group has signed the group paper. Then the messenger brings all materials to the Materials Center. Also, put the paper and observation form in the group folder that has your number on it."

"Mr. Jordan, what do we do if we didn't finish all the answers?"

"Thanks for the question, Celia. You will be back with this group tomorrow to finish your paper and begin the next section of your group's project on the section of the United States you worked on today. You will also do another teambuilding activity that we haven't done in awhile: naming your group."

There are appreciative words and smiles as students react to this announcement.

"Now, before we start rearranging the room, class, what is the next thing to do?"

"Say words of appreciation and 'Good-bye'!" chorus the students as they stand and proceed with enthusiasm.

Desks and chairs are quickly rearranged and the room soon resembles its earlier state. Cooperative learning time is over, but the cooperative spirit obviously remains.

THE FIVE UNDERLYING PRINCIPLES

Does Mr. Jordan's cooperative group experiences seem too good to be true? It is not. This is not Mr. Jordan's first experience with cooperative groups. It is almost December vacation. He has had three months in which to teach and practice cooperative learning skills with his students and this is his third year of implementing cooperative learning techniques learned in a professional development program. What occurred in Mr. Jordan's classroom was neither an accident nor a happy twist of fate. Mr. Jordan's students have learned specific social skills in a classroom environment which is based upon five important principles.

1. The Principle of Distributed Leadership

2. The Principle of Heterogeneous Grouping

3. The Principle of Positive Interdependence and Individual Accountability

4. The Principle of Social Skills Acquisition

5. The Principle of Group Autonomy

Each principle involves specific teacher behaviors which in turn can produce the desired result — student groups which demonstrate and benefit from cooperative learning skills.

1.   The Principle of Distributed Leadership

Cooperative learning is based upon the belief that all students are capable of understanding, learning and performing leadership tasks. Experience and research show that when all group members are expected to be involved and are given leadership responsibilities, we increase the likelihood that each member will be an active participant who is able to initiate leadership when appropriate.

Teacher Behavior: No leader is assigned by the teacher or chosen by the group.

Example: Mr. Jordan neither assigned group leaders in his class nor did he tell each group to choose their leader.

2. The Principle of Heterogeneous Grouping

Cooperative learning is based upon a belief that the most effective student groups are those which are heterogeneous. Groups which include students who have different social backgrounds, skill levels, physical capabilities and genders mirror the real world of encountering, appreciating and celebrating differences.

Teacher Behavior: To insure heterogeneity, the selection of groups is done randomly or group members are chosen by the teacher.

Example: The fifth graders in Mr. Jordan's class numbered off to be in randomly selected heterogeneous groups.

3. The Principle of Positive Interdependence And Individual Accountability

Cooperative learning is based upon a belief that students need to learn to recognize and value their dependence upon one another. Students who have had lots of practice working individually to complete their assignments or competitively to do better than their peers are often not initially eager to work with others. Incorporating positive interdependence increases the likelihood that students will work cooperatively

Students also need to know that they are each expected to participate, agree before work is turned in, learn, and/or master the material that is being covered. This means that they may each be required to be tested individually on the material, show what their contribution was, report on the group work, or sign the group product.

Teacher Behavior: Positive interdependence is created when the teacher employs one or more of the strategies listed below.

- Materials must be shared (limited or jigsawed).

- Group members create *one* group product.

- Group members are given a common task.

- Roles are rotated within the group during each day's work time (i.e., reader, writer, drawer, messenger).

Example: In Walter Jordan's class positive interdependence was created in the ways listed below:

- The group had only one group paper and pencil; individuals each had a different resource material.
- Students were creating a group product on the group answer sheet.
- The group's common task was for everyone to contribute, agree with the answers, and know what those answers meant.
- Each person in the group was to be a writer during work time; someone who had not had a turn being messenger was to be chosen for that role.

Teacher Behavior: The teacher holds individuals accountable after group work when one or more of the strategies listed below is employed.

- Students sign the group product. Signing shows "I participated and I agree."
- The reporter for the group (and possibly the group itself) is chosen through a lottery system.
- Each individual is responsible to demonstrate in physical, oral, or written communication his or her participation, understanding and/or mastery of the material covered.

Example: In Walter Jordan's class individual accountability was required in the following ways:

- Students were to sign the group paper.
- The group that was to report, as well as the reporter for the group itself, was randomly chosen from the "Winner's Hat."

4.   The Principle of Social Skills Acquisition

Cooperative learning is based upon a belief that the ability to work effectively in a group is determined by the acquisition of specific social skills. These social skills can be taught and can be learned.

Teacher Behavior: A teacher can teach specific cooperative social skills by defining, discussing, observing and processing with the students. In Chapters 5, 8 and 9 we will outline this procedure in step-by step detail.

Example: In Mr. Jordan's fifth grade class we observed him using these techniques when:

- A new social was defined, discussed, and specific behaviors were brainstormed for "sounds like" and "looks like."
- The social skill was practiced and observed.
- Group members processed the lesson by analyzing group behavior and reporting it to the class.

5. The Principle of Group Autonomy

Cooperative learning is based upon the belief that student groups are more likely to attempt resolution of their problems if they are not "rescued" from these problems by their teacher. When students resolve their problems with a minimum of teacher input, they become more autonomous and self-sufficient.

Teacher Behavior: Typically, because we are members of a helping profession, we intervene to help students. We try to convince them to finish a task; we settle their arguments; and we offer our solutions to their problems. As a result, we deny students the opportunity to learn from failure and from each other. In addition, we often overload ourselves as teachers to the point of exasperation or "burnout."

Unless a group oversteps the boundaries of acceptable behavior or makes a group decision to solicit teacher assistance, it is more helpful for a teacher to suggest and prompt rather than direct student activity. The teacher's role should be as observer and monitor.

Example: Mr. Jordan removed himself from direct participation in group work. He was physically available to answer group questions or interact appropriately as he moved from group to group. While he encouraged Sherry's group to explore solutions, he did not intervene with solutions of his own.

NEEDS ASSESSMENT

So far, we have examined a number of important principles and practices. We have illustrated them with Mr. Jordan's effective use of groups. You have seen the benefits of the procedures and the process.

Also, you have been introduced to the five basic principles which make cooperative groups different from typical classroom groups. We now invite you to begin gathering data for needs assessment. What do you believe about group leaders and group membership? What behaviors do you exhibit when working with groups? What modifications would you like to make? Please continue by completing the following Belief/Behavior Inventory.

1. Put an N (meaning "Now") in the ME column on the side that represents your present beliefs and behaviors.

PRINCIPLE #1 Distributed Leadership			
Cooperative Groups	**Me**		**Typical Classroom Groups**
Belief: All group members are capable of understanding, learning and performing the tasks required for a group to complete a task and like each other when the task is done.			**Belief:** One group member, chosen by the teacher or the group, is responsible for seeing that the task is completed and everyone likes each other when the job is done.
Behavior: No leader is assigned or chosen. All group members perform the leadership skills when appropriate.			**Behavior:** One leader is assigned or chosen. That leader performs all leadership skills or assigns them to group members.

PRINCIPLE #2 Heterogeneous Grouping			
Cooperative Groups	**Me**		**Typical Classroom Groups**
Belief: The most effective groups are heterogeneous in terms of social background, skill levels, physical capabilities and gender.			**Belief:** The most effective groups are homogeneous in terms of social background, skill levels, physical capabilities and gender.
Behavior: Selection of groups is made randomly or by the teacher to insure heterogeneity.			**Behavior:** The teacher selects groups based on similarities of group members.

PRINCIPLE #3 Positive Interdependence And Individual Accountability

Cooperative Groups	Me		Typical Classroom Groups
Belief: All students are not willing to work in groups unless there is a built-in reason to do so.			**Belief:** There are shared materials, one product, common goal, and/or rotated roles within the group. Each student signs group product, is prepared to report for group, and/or shows understanding or mastery of material.
Behavior: There are shared materials, one product, common goals, and/or rotated roles within the group. Each student signs group product, is prepared to report for group, and/or shows understanding or mastery of material.			**Behavior:** Group members each have own materials, make own decisions, and/or create their own product. Students are assessed based only on the product created.

PRINCIPLE #4 Social Skills Acquisition

Cooperative Groups	Me		Typical Classroom Groups
Belief: The ability to work effectively in a group comes from skills that can be taught and learned.			**Belief:** Students come to school knowing how to get along and work in groups.
Behavior: Social skills are defined, discussed, practiced, observed, and processed.			**Behavior:** Groups are told to cooperate.

PRINCIPLE #5 Group Autonomy

Cooperative Groups	Me		Typical Classroom Groups
Belief: Students learn to solve their own problems by resolving them on their own rather than being rescued from them by the teacher.			**Belief:** Group members always need the teacher's help to solve problems.
Behavior: In problem situations, the teacher suggests and prompts at the request of the entire group.			**Behavior:** The teachers directs and orders groups to solve problems according to the teacher's observations.

2. Analyze your position. If your N's are both on one side in each section, your beliefs are consistent with your behaviors. If your N's are not on the same side, you may experience stress because your beliefs and behaviors are inconsistent.

3. Now think about where you would like to be in terms of your beliefs and behaviors. We are asking you to experiment with new behaviors when you use cooperative groups, so it will be helpful for you to examine your beliefs to see if they coincide with your new practices. Go back through the columns and put an F where you would like to be in the future.

4. Look at each of the five sections again. Sometimes adjustments between beliefs and behaviors are necessary in order to avoid or reduce stress. Pick one marked with an F that you would most like to change and write an "I" statement here for yourself:

    "From now on when I work with groups, my belief is:

    _____

    _____

    so my behavior _____

    _____.

    One way I can be sure to do this is to_____

    _____

    _____."

Keep a record of your reactions as you read this book. As you notice "ah-hahs" or twinges, check back to this inventory and question yourself. Does the new information match your beliefs and behaviors? You can learn about your teaching self at the same time that you learn about cooperative groups.

GETTING STARTED: TEACHER DECISIONS

This section covers the basics of the Dishon/Wilson O'Leary model of cooperative learning, which we have refined and developed since the early 1980's. We start with this chapter on the basic teacher decisions for beginning to use cooperative learning. You will notice differences between these tips and the choices covered in the scenario about Mr. Jordan's classroom in Chapter 2. By the time you finish this guidebook, you will have an understanding of the choices he made to implement the smooth cooperative learning activity we reported.

This chapter is for teachers who have used little or no group work, as well as those who are already beginning to add cooperative learning to their repertoire of classroom techniques. It is also meant for teachers who want new ideas to enhance or improve their present practice and increase the amount of cooperative learning in their classrooms. Make choices from our ideas and suggestions based on your experience, style, and teaching philosophy.

TIPS FOR IMPLEMENTING
BEGINNING COOPERATIVE GROUPS

Successful cooperative groups begin with decisions made by the teacher carefully and consciously before students even walk into the classroom. Even though some teachers have used groups for years, some groups work better than others. We can increase the chances that groups work more effectively by making more informed conscious decisions. In this section we present five tips for implementing that include ideas we have gathered and synthesized over the years.

Tip #1. Content Application

You have plenty of content to teach now, so we won't burden you with more. We would rather you focus on cooperative learning as a method of delivering your present content objectives in a way that does more than help students "cover" the curriculum. It requires that students think and involve themselves in their learning.

We recommend that you start your implementation in only one content area or during one class period of the day. This is a gradual learning process for you and students, so begin slowly. You might also want to start with content that you and your students enjoy, if you have them for more than one period, or begin with a group of students (if you have a choice) that is your most positive, flexible, and motivated. By starting with those who are most positive, you increase the possibilities that you will have the confidence to "play" with new activities and routines. Then when you have more confidence in your abilities and how students respond, move into other content areas or include students in other class periods. By avoiding the "neediest" curriculum or students at first, you can become comfortable in tackling even the toughest content or groups.

Start with short assignments that take only 1-3 minutes to complete. The goal is to teach the routines of working together and getting work done. These first assignments get students used to talking with each other about the content, hearing experiences and information and reaching consensus. This is a first for many students, as most have learned to work alone or in competition with classmates.

If we see teachers make any "mistakes" in using cooperative learning it would be starting with groups that are too large and assignments that are too complex with no time limits. We believe it is more helpful to give students chances to work on simple tasks in a small group for short amounts of time. Assign an activity like "Turn to Your Neighbor" (see Appendix H) at the beginning of the day or class period. Ask pairs to recall or review something from a previous day's lesson such as:

- List five critical attributes of a mammal.

- Tell three characteristics of the protagonist in our play.

- Describe the steps to follow when balancing a chemical equation.

- Name 3 things in the room that are round.

Neighbors can also talk to each other in the middle of a lesson. They can clarify information or concepts, ask questions, tell the first two steps of a process.

At the end of a lesson, neighbors can discuss, practice, clarify, or summarize their learning. For example:

- Tell the difference between a synonym and antonym.
- Write in narrative form the steps you used to solve the math problems.
- Practice three declensions before the rest is done for homework.

As you move into more complex lessons that take more time, consider an amount of work that can be completed during one class session. (This includes time for giving directions and processing.) If cooperative learning is new to you, keep in mind that doing any assignment in a group will take longer than the same assignment which is done individually. If you students can do 10 math problems individually during a 20 minute work period, they probably will be able to solve five problems in a group of three during the same amount of time. It typically takes more time in a group because members must spend time to:

- Check to see that everyone understands the assigned tasks.
- Decide on a method to complete the task.
- Give everyone a turn to complete part of the task.
- Compare and agree upon answers.

Be sure to clarify for students that this is a group task. Work is not to be done individually or competitively, but cooperatively.

Quick, relatively easy tasks at the beginning of cooperative learning implementation conditions students to working in a group. Consistent and frequent practice is the key. Short tasks are easier to work into the schedule and if students aren't immediately successful, the price is not as high as it would be with longer assignments.

Tip #2. Group Composition

We know from our own experience and findings from research conducted over the years by a variety of researchers that the strongest groups are heterogeneous. That is, they contain a mixture of students who are different from one another. Differences in gender, ethnicity, experiences, skills and abilities enrich the group since there are different backgrounds, prior knowledge, opinions, etc. Notice that we did not limit differences to skill or ability level alone. Even when students are at similar skill or ability levels, there are other ways to achieve heterogeneity.

Assignment to Groups: There are several ways to decide who goes in which group. Often teachers ask us for the "magic answer" for group composition, as if groups will be sure to work if we get the right mixture of students in them! We believe that it matters less who is in the group than what was built into the group task. With that in mind, we recommend that you create group membership, at least at some times, in random ways. Names can be drawn from the "Winner's Envelope," lists of names in alphabetical order (first 3 are in one group, next 3, etc.), lists of names in chronological order of birthdays (names are listed from birthdays on January 1 to December 31; the first 3 go into one group, next 3 in a group, etc.), picking colored chips (reds go together, blues, etc.).

A more familiar way to achieve heterogeneity is to choose the groups yourself, deciding which 1 or 2 criteria you will use to compose the groups (boys/girls; students with social skills with students with fewer social skills; etc.).

You may have noticed that we have not mentioned students choosing their own groups. If you're like most teachers, your students have either begged or threatened you to let them choose their own group members. Most of us give in because we believe that at least they will do something if they make the choice. The problem is that they tend to party and socialize with their friends rather than concentrating on the task. In addition, students who don't get chosen or are the "leftovers" have their low self-esteem reinforced when this happens. These students need to be protected from this kind of rejection. Also, when students choose their own groups, they tend to be homogeneous rather than heterogeneous, usually along racial and socioeconomic lines. We also know that it *can* work to have students choose their own groups, but this happens when teachers work so hard to create an "our classroom" feeling* that their students are willing to work with anyone in the class, not just their friends.

---

*For more ideas about creating the "our classroom" feeling see Chick Moorman and Dee Dishon, *Our Classroom: We Can Learn Together,* 1983. (Available from "Cooperation Unlimited," P.O. Box 68, Portage, MI 49081.)

Because students want to know if they will ever get to work with their friends, you can assure students that some time during the semester or the year they will have worked with everyone because they will be in a variety of groups for varying lengths of time.

Acceptance of Groupmates: A major worry for some teachers is dealing with the reactions from students when groups are announced or names are pulled out of the Winner's Envelope. Cries of "Yuck!" or "Oh, no, not Celia!" can destroy a sense of safety and support among students. We recommend that you talk with students ahead of time about how it feels to get verbal or non-verbal rejection of this kind. We know of one teacher who told students "I don't let you hit one another or spit at one another in this classroom and I will not let you hurt each other with words and behaviors." This teacher was very clear that such behaviors would not be tolerated and would be met with definite consequences. Teachers have shared several other ideas with us to make sure finding out who is in which group is as positive as possible. One middle school teacher told us about the class creating cheers to welcome the announcement of names in teams. It was so unusual for students to be able to cheer in the classroom that the students really got into it and welcomed all group members.

Another technique which we highly recommend is to tell students to "act as if" they are happy about who is in their groups. This is not to deny real feelings, but to put in place behavior that is supportive. What teachers often find when students "act as if" is that they do begin to act more supportive without realizing it.

Group Size: Group size is another crucial decision that strongly impacts on group functioning and success. We have found the most effective groups are as small as 2 and no larger than 5. Our experience is that most students are not ready to work in groups larger than 2 or 3. It is easy to form "Neighbor" groups since these are students who sit next to or near each other. Using "Neighbors" takes less time and makes for less confusion because it requires little or no movement of people or furniture. If you have an uneven number of students, create one group of 3. This trio completes the same assignment that pairs do in the allotted time.

Move on to groups of three to add diversity and variety to group composition. Be wary of groups of 4 and 5. Larger groups take more time for the same work, it takes more social skills to include everyone and not have one person take control, and, frankly, it is easier to manage. This is in spite of the belief that it will be easier for teachers if they have "fewer stops to make" by creating larger groups. Teachers we work with report that smaller group size is beneficial to group success. When you have more time for students to work in groups, students' social skills have improved, and you are more comfortable with group work, it is time to increase group size to 4 or 5.

Duration of Groups: Different types of groups stay together for varying lengths of time. Neighbors might change every week. Learning Buddies are generally long-term, home base groups so they might stay together for a marking period, semester, or school year! Other groups might stay together for several weeks as they cover a specific unit of study. The idea is to have a balance so that some groups change often and one stays the same for a longer period of time.

Tip #3. Room Arrangement

Desk and room arrangement are important factors in group productivity and in maintaining your sanity. The scraping of thirty desks across the room will not endear you to your colleagues and will not help strengthen your belief that groups are a pleasant part of your instructional repertoire. Deciding how you want the room to look when students are working in cooperative groups and how you will achieve that look are pre-planning *musts*.

Consider the following:

1. Be sure group members are close together. We call this EEKK, eye-to-eye and knee-to-knee (in attitude if not actually touching body parts). You do not want a large table creating distance between students. This activity is neither labor negotiations nor a royal dinner party. Use one desk and two or three chairs, one end of a table, chairs in a tight cluster, or have students sit in a circle on the floor. Group members must be working close together facing one another to complete the subject matter task. If you have chairs with the arm attached, as in many middle and high school classrooms, consider the arrangement shown in the drawing below. As you can see, one person is seated in the "group desk" and the others are all facing him/her.

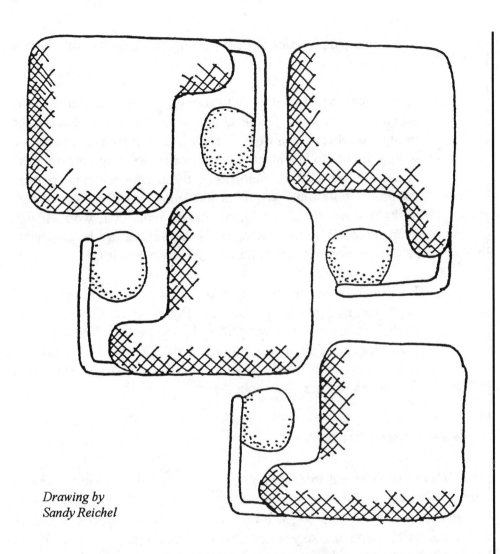

Drawing by
Sandy Reichel

You might want to consider not rearranging the room at all. That is, have students stand close together. This works well if the task is short, primarily involves talking rather than writing or drawing, and you have taught the routine of getting into standing groups and staying in the group. (See Tip #5 below, *Teach the Routine.*)

2. Be sure that all group members are on the same level. They may sit on the floor, if this is a routine in your classroom, but in the group must be on the floor. It is not acceptable for some members to be on the floor and others to be in chairs. In a cooperative group, everyone is equal; equal in place, position, and power as well as equal in opportunity to participate and learn. It is also easier for students to take over or sit out of a

group if s/he is physically above groupmates, neither of which is desirable in a cooperative group.

3. Have clear access lanes between groups since you will be moving among them. Students may also need room to leave the group to obtain classroom resources. Because conversation within the group is a must, some space between groups provides a noise buffer as well. Remember, these arrangements are **only** for group work time. We think that you can still have students' desks in rows for direct instruction or individual work. If you keep students' desks in clusters all the time, it can be unclear to students when it is appropriate to talk and when it isn't.

4. It will help keep the room calm and reduce the amount of time it takes for students to get settled if you teach the routine of moving in and out of groups. (See Tip #5 below.) If you want to help students feel ownership for how the room is arranged, consider inviting their suggestions, floor plans, etc., to help build the feeling of "our classroom."

Tip #4. Clear Directions

Have you ever had students do what you asked them to but it wasn't really what you wanted? We have and it's not pretty! To ensure that your directions are clear, we suggest that you: (1) write directions before students start group work so you can check their accuracy and clarity; and (2) post directions on the board, easel or screen during work time so that students can keep track of their own progress and understanding of the group task.

Teachers we work with find these two suggestions both helpful and difficult. Reasons they give us for the difficulty is that it takes concentration, thought, and time to do task analysis of the group's assignment. Many teachers are surprised about how clear something seems to them and how confusing it seems to students. We recommend that you ask someone else to read over your directions to check whether or not students would know what to do.

Most teachers avoid writing up directions because it takes time and planning, and they don't believe that students need directions written up. We have heard a wide range of reasons.

- ◆ "I want them to learn to follow oral directions." This is fine if you want to answer questions all over the room. Many of your students are visual learners and will be helped by actually seeing the directions. Also, since a desired outcome of group work is that students will get deeply involved in the task, this will be more difficult if they don't remember what they are to do next.

- ◆ "My students are too young (or unskilled) to read directions anyway." We know the importance of surrounding non-readers with the written word. Where better to have this "code" displayed than on directions that the teacher has gone over with them beforehand.

- ◆ "I just don't have the materials or the time to write up the directions." We know teachers who are so clear about the benefits of writing up directions for students they will say "Paper" rather than "Plastic" in the checkout line at the grocery store so they can tear open the grocery bag, write up the directions, and tape them to the chalkboard. Otherwise, write directions on the chalkboard, easel, or on a transparency to be displayed on a screen.

We have found that once teachers try writing up directions, they are so pleased with the results of group work that they make it a part of all group lessons.

The good news, too, about posting written directions is that when students have learned the routine, the directions do not need to be posted because with very few oral directions, they know what to do.

It is important to tell students how much work time they have and include that information in the written directions. If you leave the amount of time indefinite, you may find what we have: students typically do not get to work until the teacher is nearby or until they are warned or told that time is up! If you give two minutes to work, for example, use a stopwatch or timer, and then stick to that amount of time, students begin to learn that: (1) they can get a lot done in two minutes; and (2) you mean what you say! It is important to train students in use of time instead of letting them train you to always give them a little more time! Don't warn or add more time so that students learn to keep track of time, get themselves to work, and refocus themselves on the task when groupmates wander off physically or mentally. This will not be easy and you won't always guess right about the amount of time needed. Just hang in there and it will get easier with practice.

Tip #5. Routines

The key to consistent implementation is to establish routines for cooperation. We define a routine as a set of behaviors which are practiced and repeated to establish and maintain effective management.

To teach a routine:

1. Name the routine.

2. State rationale for the routine and expected behaviors.

3. Model the behavior.

4. Practice.

5. Process student perceptions of success with practice.

6. Give feedback on accuracy of the behavior.

For example, in teaching the Quiet Signal, the teacher needs to tell students what it is, why it's needed and how it will look and sound. When we teach the Quiet Signal, we tell students that they will be busy working and talking in groups and at some point we will want their attention. When the teacher holds up his or her hand, students who are not speaking are to raise their hand, keep listening, and not say anything else. The person who is talking is to finish the sentence and then raise his/her hand to pass on the signal. Students are then given a chance to practice by being stopped and started as they talk in groups. They can be asked how they thought they did. "Did the person who was speaking when the Quiet Signal was noticed finish the sentence?" "How can you make sure that the person talking finishes the sentence and doesn't start another one?" Last, the teacher may give his/her opinion about how s/he perceived the accuracy of the behaviors, noting such things as hands up and people still talking. Cooperative learning becomes quicker and easier as all of the above mentioned tips become routines.

Summary

It may seem like there are a lot of decisions to make before cooperative groups will work smoothly in your classroom. That's because there are! However, just as students will establish routines with practice and processing, so will you. As these decisions become part of your repertoire, you will be able to make them quickly on the spur of the moment.

THREE-STEP
COOPERATIVE LEARNING LESSON

We have created a 3-step framework on which to build cooperative group activities. No matter how simple or how complex the content or activity, these components need to be present. This framework helps you employ these tips as well as the critical attributes of a cooperative learning strategy.

    I.   Subject Matter Directions

        Positive Interdependence

        Individual Accountability

        Face-to-face interaction

    II. Teacher Monitors

    III. Process Subject Matter

        Hear Responses

        See Products

        Correct Work

        Discuss Academic Skills

I. Subject Matter Directions. Before group work, students need to know what they are to accomplish. State what students are to discuss, write, draw, solve, color, cut, paste, play, sing. Effective directions include the components of positive interdependence and individual accountability, which are the built-in reasons for students to work together. (See Chapter 4 for specifics.) Decisions need to be made about materials being shared and/or jigsawed; one product being created; which jobs needed to be rotated within the group (positive interdependence). In addition, students will either be randomly chosen to report about the group's work, demonstrate what happened, and/or take a quiz to show their understanding or competence (individual accountability).

Students also need to know where they are to work with their group for this particular assignment (see Tip #3 above). Groups have a difficult time functioning efficiently if students are not facing one another on the same level. You will also want students close together to keep down the noise that is a natural result of students talking in groups. The closer together they are, the more softly they tend to talk. This proximity also helps everyone in the group to be able to see the group's book, paper, map, picture, etc.

Directions can be more easily given if students are seated in their own places rather than already in their groups. When students are grouped at the front of the room or in rows, their attention is more easily focused toward the front of the room where you are reading the posted directions. When you have checked for understanding with students (oral response, signals, etc.), it is time to give the signal to move to groups. We use the word "Go!" You can decide your own verbal or non-verbal signal.

II. Teacher Monitors. During group work, your job is to walk around and observe group work in action. Notice what students are doing with the content. Look at what they are drawing or writing. Collect ideas about what needs to reviewed, retaught, skipped, highlighted. Walk around. Listen to each group's conversation.

This is not the time to become a part of any group. It is tempting to join groups to prompt or praise, to cajole or encourage. We recommend that you tell students that you are "invisible" and that you will only become visible when they ask a group question.

A group question is one that each member of the group agrees they cannot answer or they have more than one answer and only one can be right. The signal is given (flag up, hands all raised), then when you go over to the group you say "Is this a group question?" When you get the affirmative, call on one person in the group to ask the question. If this person does not know what the question is or the others say, "That's not the question" tell students you will be happy to help them as soon as it is a *group* question. You will need to teach the routine of the group question, since students are very used to asking questions whenever they want and we are well trained to answer each and every one! The point here is not to trick students, but rather to be unnoticed as students work so they only look to you when it is necessary.

This does not, of course, mean that the teacher never interrupts a group. It means that you consciously decide whether or not to intervene in a group. Intervene if you see or hear incorrect practice, students teaching incorrect information, or students not using content correctly. Interrupt a group if students are hurting one another physically or emotionally and tell them that you will do so. (For more about teacher's role, see Chapter 7.)

It is tempting to go back to your desk and get to the piles of paperwork while students are busily working in their groups. Please do not give into that temptation. When you are visibly peering into groups, you send the important message that group work is essential. Group assignments are not just used for busy work so you can get other jobs done, as some teachers and students erroneously assume. Use this time to gather data about social interactions and student learning without having to correct more papers or tests! Watch and listen to get data that is available now!

III. Process Subject Matter. Group work time is done. It must be time to pack up and go to the next subject, next class, or home. Right? No. It is time to process. In the Dishon/Wilson O'Leary model, "process the subject matter" means that something needs to be done with the experience and/or group products. Part of planning the lesson is to decide what you will do with the knowledge, skills, and products. Reflect that plan in your subject matter directions (Step I). Carry out your plan at the end of group work.

Set aside 3-8 minutes to look at how students worked together on the task and/or to see/hear their group products or results. Ask students questions about the process they used to complete the project, collect information, etc. (See Appendix F for subject matter processing statements.) Call on some or all of the students to report their findings to the rest of the class. You may correct the products as a class or you may do that later on your own. Collect the products. If you want students to take group work seriously, you have to take the fruits of their work time seriously. This means that you need to spend time examining the process of the group's academic thinking as well as hold individuals accountable for participation.

With this 3-step framework, it is possible to take an activity and thoughtfully plan a well structured cooperative learning lesson.

Cooperative Strategies

We include 13 activities that we have created and adapted that can be used in many content areas and grade levels. Read through them (Appendix H) with your grade level or subject matter objectives in mind and decide which might work for you and your students. Mix and match with your content area(s) to create frequent, consistent opportunities for cooperative groups. (We have listed the titles below for your information.)

1. Turn to Your Neighbor

2. Think-Pair-Share

3. Pairs of Pairs

4. Advanced Pairs of Pairs

5. Learning Buddies

6. Show & Tell / Bring & Brag

7. Dynamic Discussions

8. Pairs and Practice

9. Jigsaw

10. Team Practice & Drill

11. Numbered Heads Together

12. Getting to Know Us

13. Groups and Homework

How to Introduce to Students

There may be times when you want to jump directly into group work without explaining or doing any sort of introduction. We believe that cooperative groups are more effective if there is some plan, so choose one or more of these ideas, then jump into group work.

If you are worried about the strong antisocial behaviors in your classroom, you may want to frequently use a variety of these suggestions, as well as discussions of the need for getting along with others. (See Chapter 9 on processing social skills.)

If you have used groups consistently in the past but now want students to be more cooperative, your class discussions might be brief and be only a point of focus.

- Use some sort of audiovisual aid. Show some pictures or posters that represent people cooperating or helping each other. Write quotations or sayings on the easel or chalkboard that remind students of experiences of friendship or cooperation. Sing a song about cooperation. Make it a "round" that requires groups of students to sing in patterns with each other.

- Use a metaphor to stimulate the association of cooperation with real-life situations. We like the examples of a car pool, geese flying in V formation, two people paddling a canoe, different types of sports teams. Pick one or more that fits the ages and interests of your students or make up your own.

- Plan a demonstration or role-play how people work well in a group or typical problems in groups and ways they can be solved.

- Invite a guest speaker from government or business to come into your room and tell about the need for cooperation in the work place.

- Provide or ask students for samples of cooperation from current events, literature, sciences, history, etc. Use your subject matter to point out the human tendency to cooperate.

- Give a brief lecture of 25 words or less! State your reasons why it is important that your students learn to work in groups. Keep it short and appropriate to YOUR student's developmental and interest level.

Whatever your situation, use these ideas, or make up your own, as a starting point for discussion. Ask students for their experience with cooperation, the lack of cooperation, their feelings when cooperation happens and their perceptions of the need for cooperation in the classroom, school, family, community, state, nation, world. Such a framework can help students understand why you are insisting that they learn to work together so clue them in!

Set Expectations

We suggest that you begin group work with very clearly stated guidelines. It is helpful to post these guidelines in the room as a constant reminder. You can suggest a starter list and ask students for their input to complete the list. Review it frequently. Add to or delete from as the class agrees.

Sample guidelines:

♦ Stay with your group.

♦ Group questions only. (See Chapter 7, *Teacher's Role During Work Time.*)

♦ Use only encouraging words (no put-downs).

♦ "Act as if" you are interested, like people in your group, etc.

♦ Include and help everyone in your group.

Team Building Activities

We believe that team building is essential when beginning to use group work or when creating new groups. It is best done frequently at the beginning to help students get to know each other on a more personal level. In large schools students might only know the people who sit near them or who are in their reading group or ride their bus. In small schools students might know one another's names and even family members, but only by reputation. In a cooperative classroom and cooperative group, we want students to be known, accepted, and appreciated for who they are right now, not last year or last semester.

Students feeling like a team doesn't happen by chance. Team building activities must be built into your classroom routine. We have included a sample collection of team building activities that we have adapted in Appendix I. We make these recommendations to you whether you use activities we have supplied, ones you presently enjoy using, ones you used to use but had forgotten about, ones you collect from colleagues.

After each teambuilding activity, ask several groups to report responses to the whole class. This helps build a sense of "our classroom" as students get to know classmates in other groups. Reporters may be volunteers or randomly chosen. You may want to have *each* group report IF there is interest and you are willing to take the time.

- ◆ Team building activities are meant to include, not exclude, so be sure to speak up when you notice behaviors that indicate competition or judgment of other's responses.
- ◆ These activities are short. They do not take a whole class period or morning. Keep them short and you can include them more frequently.
- ◆ It is more advantageous to have short, frequent activities all semester or year than to have only one or two longer activities at the beginning of the school year.
- ◆ While a group can get together for just a team building activity, usually a short team builder precedes a content assignment. One of the purposes of a cooperative group is to teach getting along and working with others as well as to help students learn subject matter.

Creating the Cooperative Classroom

Cooperative learning does not happen in isolation from what occurs in the classroom before or after group work. Students may treat each other politely during group time, but spit at each other, literally or figuratively, at other times during the school day or class period. If you want to build a cooperative classroom, (also called the "our classroom" in this guidebook and the subject for *Our Classroom: We Can Learn Together* listed in the bibliography), in which cooperative groups are a delivery system for subject matter and social skills, we suggest that you include cooperative goals and expectations within your classroom.

Behaviors that promote cooperation:

- Scores or grades are given to the teacher individually, not called out in the classroom.

- Appreciation is given to groups or individuals for correct, carefully prepared work, and not for finishing first.

- Bulletin boards are titled "We" and "Our." Examples: "The Titles of Books WE Have Read"; "OUR Classroom Rules"; "OUR Favorite Papers"; etc.

- Each school day of the month students give the teacher something to write: birthdays, teeth lost, guest helpers present, field trip, weather reports, etc. Those papers are dated and hung in chronological order on the bulletin board. At the end of the month the pages are put in a scrapbook for students to refer to: "Look at How Busy We Were in January," for example.

- Local history is required in some classrooms. Students bring something for the bulletin board. It may be an old photograph with an explanation, family tree information, an anecdote written down by or from a family member or friend, or something the students have researched in the library. This creates a feeling of living, cooperative history in the classroom.

- Groups help other groups when finished and asked.

- "Treasure Hunt" or "Bingo" activities for get-acquainted or content review are done with the goal of "Help everyone finish correctly."

(The above ideas quoted from *Cooperation Unlimited Ink,* vol. 6, #1, Fall 1992, pages 1-3.)

We ask you to watch your behavior and listen to your words as you interact with students and adults during the school day. Is cooperation your goal? Every word and action counts as students observe how you "walk your talk."

Four Steps in Learning a New Skill

We assume that whatever you have done with group work in the past reflected your best efforts. We do not assume that you have been doing anything wrong with groups. So why do we want you to make all of these decisions and changes? We have made cooperative groups our focus for many years and think we can help you avoid some of the bruises and lacerations we have experienced. We offer you our suggestions to help speed up your process of assimilation and success. We have learned as teachers and parents, however, that we cannot, and would not want to, do it all for you.

When you are dedicated to change for any reason (self-development, student learning, building or district goals, etc.), you go through several steps along the way.

1. **Unconsciously unskillful (unawareness).** You have used groups and called them cooperative. Some days they were and other days they weren't. You have read journal articles and books and attended workshops. Now you are reading this guidebook. Until now you have been unaware of what we, Dee and Pat, call cooperative learning.

2. **Consciously unskillful (awareness and frustration).** At this step you have taken some of our suggestions and tried some lessons. Some went well and, frankly, some didn't. It would be easy to slip back to your former methods, maybe using cooperative learning and maybe not. It's a natural phase of growth. "If it isn't going to work perfectly every time, I won't bother." We know the feeling. However, we ask you to buck up and keep going. Hang in there. Keep the groups heterogeneous. Pick the groups yourself or use random selection. Don't let students whining, apathy, or challenges get you down. In the long run these methods will work. Trust the model.

3. **Consciously skillful (planned success).** The way to increase the success of cooperative groups is to increase the conscious, detailed planning. When a cooperative group lesson works well, we know it is because you included the appropriate components. When a cooperative group lesson doesn't go well, we can bet that you can look back at this chapter and notice what components got left out of the planning.

    We also know that there is frustration at this step because as a professional you are used to making decisions on your feet. Here we are asking you to make decisions on your seat, before class time. This is a twist that can take you outside of your comfort zone.

The planning takes time and effort. If you are going to take on this model, you need to recognize this and be willing to pay the price. Remember, the reward will be more positive and productive groups more often. After routines are established, the time spent in planning will be reduced.

4. **Unconsciously skillful (routine).** This is where most of us as professionals are used to working: at the comfortable level of routine. You will know that you and your students are there when you say: "Get into your math groups," and everyone moves quickly and quietly; when students know that you only answer groups questions; when you pull a group task "out of the air" knowing that you can put the components in place in moments. You will reach that level of comfort with this model of cooperative learning, too. It takes time and commitment.

Some teachers tell us that they get comfortable with the details quickly, sometimes within two to three weeks. Others tell us it takes them months or a whole school year. Some staff developers say that it takes two or three years (as you have probably noticed when changing grade levels or adopting new textbooks).

We agree that changing the way you use group work is a process. It involves decision-making, activities, reflection, and more decision-making based on your experiences. Don't expect immediate, complete success. Do keep track of the small, continuous signs of success. They add up and make the effort worthwhile.

Start Now!

"I think I'll just wait until the start of next school year."

"If only I had started on the first day of the semester, things would be easier."

"How can we start this in November? Winter vacation is in a few weeks."

There are many teachers who tell us that it is best to start cooperative learning in the beginning of the year, the semester, the unit, etc. We agree AND we believe that today is the first day of the rest of the school year, even if it is May 10. Begin as soon as you read this book, attend a cooperative learning workshop, have students to teach. If you are at the beginning of the year, yes, you can start routines upon which to build all year. If you are at the beginning of a semester, the students think that groups are just what you use all of the time. On the other hand, if it is near a vacation time (summer, winter, spring), you might as well use group work since not much else works at those times of the year anyway! To begin cooperative learning is the same as beginning a diet or exercise program: it's never too late and you can't begin soon enough.

In this chapter we have given you many ways to get started using cooperative groups in your classroom. Don't become overwhelmed with all of the choices. Just start. Pick three or four things from the chapter to implement soon. Set a day of the week and an hour of the day to begin. Practice the techniques consistently. Add a new Cooperative Strategy every week for the next month. Keep using the old favorites in new content areas or with new groups. Be kind to yourself and your students. Have fun!

POSITIVE INTERDEPENDENCE
AND
INDIVIDUAL ACCOUNTABILITY

Teachers in our workshops and classes who have used little or no group work, often fantasize about how much their students will enjoy working in cooperative groups. They are sure that young people who take every opportunity to interact in the classroom will be delighted to finally have legitimate reasons to work together. They are convinced that students will enthusiastically move into group work because working with others would appear to be more fun than working alone. Consequently, one of the biggest surprises for teachers beginning to use cooperative groups is that these fantasies are not always true. Some students want to work only in a group with friends of their own choosing. Others prefer to work alone. Still others would rather not do any work at all.

Teachers who have done a lot of group work tend to ask questions that indicate they know that many students are not willing to work in a group with just anyone. The teachers are mystified by how to keep some students from taking over a group and others from sitting back and letting others do all of the work. They practically demand to know how to motivate students to work together.

Some students prefer to work alone because they have been trained that way. Teachers have taught students to "Look at your own paper," "Don't tell anyone the answer," and that "Sharing answers is cheating." The "bad news" is that students have successfully learned to operate from such an "I, me, my" perspective. *"I* have to do *my* work at *my* desk." The "good news" is that students can be taught to adopt an "Us, we, our" stance so that during cooperative group work, words like *"We* have to finish *our* paper and be sure that *everyone* signs it," are easy to say, believe, and act out.

This re-teaching involves more than wishing students would work together or crossing our fingers hoping for a group that is willing to

CHAPTER 4

cooperate. More than luck, the full moon, or magic is necessary. It requires a conscious and continuous effort to structure reasons for students to work together. It requires *positive interdependence*.

POSITIVE INTERDEPENDENCE

Positive interdependence is a term that describes the relationship between members of a cooperative group. Students in a cooperative group succeed only if every member of the group succeeds. If one fails, they all fail. They are positively interdependent because, in order for everyone to be successful, they must care about whether or not *all* their group members are successful, or at least act as if they do. This is commonly called "We sink or swim together."

Initially, most students do not automatically care about the others in the group. For that reason, this relationship must be encouraged by the teacher. We often define positive interdependence as extrinsic reasons for students to work together. We know that with the right ingredients, these purely extrinsic reasons become intrinsic as behaviors change and many students genuinely want themselves and their groupmates to be successful.

When positive interdependence is in place in groups, these are typical behaviors:

- Students stay with their group.
- Students talk about the task.
- Materials are shared.
- Answers and information are shared.
- Students check with each other on the material.
- Others watch as one person at a time writes.
- Heads are close together over the group's paper.

When positive interdependence is *not* in place, these behaviors are typical:

- Students leave their group without the group's permission.
- Students talk, but not about the task.
- Students protect their answers and do not share.

- No one checks to see if others have learned or understand the material.

- Each person is writing.

- People lean back, working independently or not working, uninvolved in the group effort.

Specific strategies that encourage students to "care" about their groupmates are needed to support desired cooperative group outcomes.

POSITIVE INTERDEPENDENCE: BUILDING IN EXTRINSIC MOTIVATORS

By carefully designing a lesson to include any or all of the following methods of positive interdependence, students can be invited to pull together and work as a team: limited materials; jigsawed materials; common goal; one product; rotate roles.

Limited Materials

This method means that there are fewer materials than there are group members. For example, instead of three pencils for a group of 3, there is only one. Instead of three identical worksheets to complete, there is one. Rulers, scissors, poster board, and dictionaries are other examples of materials that can be limited. In Mr. Jordan's classroom (Chapter 2), each group received only *one* group paper and *one* group pencil.

When each student has his or her own paper and pencil, the group looks very different from one in which there is *one* piece of paper and *one* pencil. In the former situation, everyone sits back and does his or her own work — there is little interaction. In the latter situation, group members are seen with their heads together over the paper as one person uses the pencil. Students can clearly be seen leaning into the experience and even bumping heads if they are not careful.

We believe that limiting materials is the most crucial method of building in positive interdependence. It is possible, however, to build in all five methods, which makes it more difficult for students to take over a group or stay out of a group.

Samples of Materials That Can Be Limited
(fewer items than there are group members)

Pencil	Protractor
Crayons	Typewriter
Textbook	Thesaurus
Answer sheet	Sewing machine
Ruler	Fabric
Paper	Template
Scissors	Triangle
Dictionary	Glue
Map	Roll of tape
Compass	Clay
Periodic chart of elements	Basketball
Computer	Soccer ball

Jigsawed Materials

This method involves dividing up the work or materials so that each group member has a part. No one has everything that is needed to complete the task. In Mr. Jordan's classroom (Chapter 2), each student had a different type of reference book.

Jigsawing can also be used when students are doing research for a report. Each member of the group is assigned a part of a famous person's life, an aspect of a war, or the events leading to a discovery.

Another method of jigsawing is to divide an assignment so that each group member does a part. For example, if the group's assignment is to write the definitions, phonetic spellings and sentences for a list of words, three steps are involved. 1) The group or teacher divides the assignment so everyone has a part. 2) Each does his/her own part, away from the group. 3) Each brings his/her part back to the group, contributing his/her part to the group product, teaching his/her information to groupmates. Everyone in the group is responsible for knowing all parts of the assignment.

Materials can also be jigsawed for primary students. In a first grade class which we observed, three students were responsible for working together to put three pictures in chronological order. Each student had one of the pictures and all three pictures had to be used to complete the sequence. In another class, three kindergartners were drawing a picture requiring the use of six different colored crayons. Because each student had two crayons with which he or she could color, each person's materials were essential for completion of the product.

Samples of Materials That Can Be Jigsawed
(group members have different materials or parts of the work)

Words	Sections of report
Pictures	Parts of puzzle
Definitions	Homework problems
Colored markers/crayons	Art supplies
Resource books	Sewing supplies
Definitions	Parts of directions
Drafting tools	Ingredients for cooking
Lab equipment	Rules for game

One product

Another way to build in positive interdependence is to be sure that students focus on creation of *one* product rather than on individual products. Students create *one* list of: topics for research; activities on the playground that include everyone; objects in the room that are triangles; animals that are mammals; synonyms; list of questions for Friday quiz; ways to solve a math problem. Students create *one:* story; picture; diorama; mural; list. When only one product is created, there is the necessity for cooperation if the group is to be successful. Some people complain that if students create only one product, only one student will do everything and some will do nothing. The problem with everyone creating his or her own product is that there will be little or no cooperation. The objective is the discussion of information and the decision-making, rather than just the product. The solution is to build in other methods of positive interdependence or individual accountability (see below), rather than avoiding this method.

Common goal

Often students do not create a product in cooperative groups; instead they make sure that everyone: studies; learns; reads; shares; tells; chooses; contributes. In this case, it is essential that students are absolutely clear that everyone is to be involved. Some teachers will even build in creation of a product when the common goal is only to discuss a specific question. One high school geometry teacher we know had students fill out an "Exit Pass" which was half a sheet of paper that each pair of neighbors had to write on whenever the teacher said "Turn to your neighbor, tell and then write: what is the next step; list the first two steps in solving this problem; what are three possible theorems that could be used in this proof?" Students had to agree on a response, write it down, and then prepare both students to tell what their answer was. At the end of the class period, each neighbor had to sign the Exit Pass and bring it "as a 4-legged creature" to the teacher in order to leave the class. The point was to show students that this was important work AND the teacher did not have to check papers, enter scores into the grade book, etc. The teacher was surprised, however, to find that she learned a lot about what students did and didn't know about the geometry unit they were on. She valued being able to "monitor and adjust" immediately, instead of waiting until after Friday quiz or the unit test.

Rotate Roles

There are many jobs to be done in a group in order for it to be successful. When considering roles in cooperative groups, we prefer to use roles that refer more to mechanics than status: reader; writer; messenger; drawer; proofreader; etc. Instead of giving each person in the group a specific role, as we recommended in the first edition of *A Guidebook For Cooperative Learning,* teachers we work with find it more helpful for students to take turns performing each role. Instead of one person doing all of the writing in the group, for example, the group pencil is passed around so each person has a turn. Instead of one person doing all of the reading, each person is required to do some part of it. We have found that in most groups, students will tend to have the best writer write, the best reader read, the best artist draw, etc. The problem is that the designated writer, reader, artist is the one person who typically needs the LEAST practice. Everyone in the group deserves the chance to be equally involved with the group, giving encouragement, support, and help if necessary.

INDIVIDUAL ACCOUNTABILITY
AFTER GROUP WORK

Individual accountability refers to the necessity of the teacher having some idea of how involved each student was in the group's work. S/he needs ways to check individuals after their group work time for participation, understanding, or mastery, depending on the common goal. Individual accountability can also help students determine their success in the group. If everyone can say they have been involved, or know the material, or have mastered a skill, then the group can feel successful. If, however, everyone has not been involved or has failed to master his/her part, the group needs to feel the responsibility to include that group member more often and help her/him.

We recommend these three ways to hold students individually accountable for what happened in the group: signatures; random check; individual performance.

Signatures

Much attention has been given to the quality of products made in the United States. We notice in many areas that when workers sign their names to products it seems to help them have a sense of responsibility, so they take the credit for successful work and the blame if they produce an inferior product.

Students need to know before group work begins that each will be signing the group product at the end of group work time. Signing means "I participated and I agree with what is here." There is typically some pressure on students who don't want to work in the group to do so because all groupmates know that even that person will have to sign.

Teachers of very young students report that when youngsters understand the importance of signatures, they take this very seriously. They learn not to sign ahead of time (it's like signing a blank check!) and they also learn not to sign someone else's name (forgery will get you 5-10 years in prison!). Even the Supreme Court gets a minority opinion, so of course a student *could* sign only the part of the group report with which s/he does agree.

Random Check

Lots of times teachers say to students, "I will call on someone randomly to answer the question." We know from experience and the research that calling randomly on students is not possible *unless* some lottery system is employed. One method that teachers of all grade levels use and enjoy is the random check method we call "Winner's Envelope." Actually the container can be a basket, a box, a can, a beaker in the science lab! Everyone's name is on a popsicle stick, tongue depressor, ticket, piece of paper, or checker so when it's time to call on someone, one of the items is drawn to determine who will answer. The point is to be sure that students know it's "fair" and that anyone could be called on at any time whether they are male or female, gifted or remedial, rich or poor, motivated or napping, etc. Using the Winner's Envelope helps raise the learner's "level of concern" which helps increase motivation. Even when one groupmate is not particularly interested in the possibility of public response, other group members can often put on enough pressure to get this student on board.

Individual Performance

Many teachers appreciate the benefits of group work and at the same time feel a concern about whether or not individual group members are pulling their own weight. Checking to determine whether students have participated, learned the material, and/or reached mastery is an essential part of many cooperative group activities. Teachers may *hear* an oral response from each student (i.e., recite numerals from 1-10), *see* a demonstration from each student (each sets up lab equipment for a different part of the experiment), or *check* an individual quiz or test from each student (i.e., individuals write a paragraph after group study and practice of the form of a well-written paragraph). Because each student is tested individually, each student receives her/his individual check, percent, grade, etc.

Just the mention of grades and cooperative learning raises serious questions and concerns in the minds of even the most ardent cooperative learning advocates. Even though in our first edition of the *Guidebook* we recommended using group grades, we now tell teachers to avoid them since the whole issue of group grades has created much confusion and in some cases damaged the cause of cooperative learning. There are teachers who have refused to support cooperative learning because of thoughtless use of group grades by educators who assign a group project and a group grade without understanding the necessity of building in positive interdependence and individual accountability. Our stance now is — DON'T GIVE GROUP GRADES!!

Types of grading that fit our definition of group grades are: averaging scores of groupmates' individual papers or tests; the grade on one paper chosen at random is the grade for all groupmates; the group product receives a grade that all groupmates receive. Remember, do not use these!

Grading in general brings up both practical and philosophical questions. Does everything students create need to be graded? If grades are not given, what will motivate students to work on the assignment? Also, if everything cannot be tested, how does the teacher know how involved students were in the group activity: who did what; who did the most; who did the least?

We believe that not every product created or practice that students perform should be graded. If students are not motivated unless a grade is given, it's time for teachers to look at the work they're assigning and make it more interesting and relevant! It is also possible to give grades or credit for individual work that a student brings to a group activity, with only a "Satisfactory" or "Unsatisfactory" for the product created by the group.

On large projects (mural, diorama, report on pyramids, etc.) there are ways to keep track of individual contributions and whether or not obligations were met in a satisfactory way. An example of one plan is the following.

Sample Time Line for Research Report

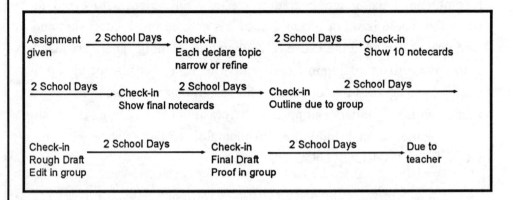

Assignments are made to individuals by the group or the teacher. Groups meet two or three times each week of the assignment. At each meeting the individuals must show the group evidence of their work (book they're reading, note cards they have written, etc.)

During check-in, the teacher is available to answer group questions, observe progress, and make notes to follow up later. Group members are to encourage, support, remind, and motivate one another. At the beginning of this process, time spent in groups is short, from 4-6 minutes. Each student shows the product assigned. Students can clarify the process for those who are unclear or the teacher can be called on for clarification. When it is time for editing and proofing, the group will need a longer work time to get to everyone's paper.

Rewards

Some teachers build in a sense of students caring about their groupmates by giving a reward for a satisfactory score on test, product, etc. There is an ongoing debate in the cooperative learning community about using rewards. On one end of the continuum is Robert Slavin who says that students need a reward every time they complete a product; Alfie Kohn is on the other end of the continuum and contends that students should never receive even teacher praise for group work (see resources)! We are somewhere between these two points of view because we know that some teachers still punish students when they are not successful, and we believe that giving a reward is more positive and motivating than punishment.

Rewards are motivators that increase the chances that students will work together in a more positive manner than they did without the reward. Several conditions need to be in place before rewards are offered to students.

Conditions for Use of Rewards

1) Rewards can be offered as a last resort when students are *extremely* resistant to working together and the teacher has consistently included team building, positive interdependence, individual accountability, social skills, and processing (see Chapters 3, 4, 8 and 9).

2) Rewards are based on pre-set, observable criterion which is announced to students before group work. We recommend setting a criterion low enough so that every group has a chance to reach it and high enough so that each group has to work to achieve it. This might be 70-90% depending on the material and the students' familiarity with it. If you decide that reaching criterion means getting 100%, then the work should be a review of something you believe all students have learned. Some teachers find that if the criterion for satisfactory group work is 100%, some groups may give up because they are unable to reach it. If the work is too easy, groups may complete the task too quickly and not feel challenged. A reasonable criterion is one that requires groups to spend sufficient time on the work and yet provides a range of acceptability that is possible to attain. A criterion may be set for the group to reach, or it might be that each person in the group has her or his individual criterion. A skilled speller may have to achieve 95% on a spelling test, an average speller 85%, and a less skilled speller 70% to reach criterion. Whatever the criteria, be sure that students are informed ahead of time and that your expectations are clear.

3) Everyone in the group gets the reward or no one does.

4) There is no competition between groups to get the reward; all groups which reach the pre-set criterion can get the reward.

5) No grades used as motivators.

6) Bonus points are not applied to grades.

Warnings for Use of Rewards

There are some dangers inherent in offering rewards to students. Teachers who assign repetitive, lower level thinking tasks often have to use rewards to motivate students to persevere. The solution is more higher-level, interesting, relevant, interactive activities. Another danger is that students can become addicted to the reward. It can create the "What are you doing to pay me?" syndrome. There is also a growing body of evidence in the research that giving rewards for group work interferes with learning for intrinsic reasons.

Possible Rewards
(To be used only with the guidelines and warnings in this chapter.)

Recognition for Elementary Students:	Middle School Students:	High School Students:
Happy Grams to students; parents; principal	Happy Grams to students; parents; principal	Recognition in daily announcements
Students of the week	Students of the week	Display work
Recognition in daily announcements	Display work	Standing ovation
Smiles	Round of applause	Round of applause
Pats on back	Encouraging words	Encouraging words

Privileges for Elementary Students:	Middle School Students:	High School Students:
Extra recess	Choose where to sit	Library passes
Stay in at recess	Work in hall	Allowed to do homework in class
Silent reading time	Gum chewing	Computer time
Help teacher	Computer time	Early to lunch on special day
Run errands	Early to lunch on special day	Choice of background music
Choose the day's story		

Tangible Rewards for Elementary Students:	Middle School Students:	High School Students:
Stars	Grab bag of prizes	Pencils
Stickers	Stickers	Bonus points
Grab bag of prizes	Free passes to athletic event or dance	Free passes to athletic event or dance
Pencils	Bonus points	Video game tokens

As you can see from these lists, we include the reward of "bonus points." Bonus points are usually a concrete item (certificate or ticket) which bears the owner's name. They are saved and turned in for privileges or items. In some classrooms, bonus points are collected until the owner has enough accumulated to turn in for such things as a one-day extension pass, water pass (can get drink), etc. (Students keep track of their own bonus points, so if they are misplaced or lost it is a loss only to the person who owns them; the teacher should definitely *not* take over this responsibility.)

Teachers have also found that students can be highly motivated by a "chance" card. This is like a lottery ticket that goes into the lottery box. When a drawing is conducted, the winner gets a prize. (Teachers report that it doesn't even matter what it is; students just love winning *something*.) This meets all of the above criteria because anyone can win since the more times your group is successful, the more lottery tickets you have in the drawing. One high school teacher we know added a twist that we found interesting. A drawing was conducted once a week, you had to be present to win, and no one knew what day of the week the lottery would take place! It was unbelievable how many students showed up in class on the chance that it was lottery day!

We have found that the best rewards are the ones your students brainstorm that they would like to have. After you approve of all the ones that are ethical, legal and fit your comfort level, you will have a list that can be very motivating to your students.

There is a danger in taking this much space to discuss rewards. Many people will think we advocate their use. Rewards are only to be used when it's time to "break glass in case of emergency!" Use them only for a short time and then eliminate.

Intrinsic Motivation

Building in external reasons for students to cooperate can lead to internal motivation to work in groups. Students exhibit intrinsic motivation when they need no rewards, motivators, or reminders about how to work in a group. When given a task to do, they do it with energy and enthusiasm. Students talk to one another, receive input from everyone in the group, share ideas and create a positive rewarding experience for themselves. We call this the "Mount Everest Theory" which describes why groups work on a task when there is no reward or individual accountability. Just as mountain climbers explain why they want to climb Mount Everest ("just because it's there"), each group works on a task just because it is there.

There are no guarantees as to how long it takes students to reach this stage. It could take some students just a few sessions and others a few months. Your students will grow towards internal motivation as you give them more opportunities to work together and solve their problems independently.

REDUCING PROBLEM BEHAVIORS
THROUGH POSITIVE INTERDEPENDENCE

As you observe your students working in groups, you may have noticed some unhelpful behaviors that occur again and again. You notice that in spite of regularly scheduled team building activities (Chapter 3), consistent processing sessions (Chapter 9) and after assigning new social skills (Chapter 8), negative behaviors continue. To help you recognize and diagnose these behaviors, we have divided the most common ones into four categories of behavior. In this section we describe these behaviors and suggest how specific strategies for creating positive interdependence can be used in each situation. If you recognize any of these behaviors as problems in your classroom or with any of your classes, you may want to incorporate one of the suggested strategies into your next cooperative group lesson.

Passive Uninvolvement

Typical Behaviors:

- Turning away from the group
- Not participating
- Not paying attention to the work
- Saying little or nothing
- Showing no enthusiasm
- Not bringing work or materials

Suggested Strategies:

- Jigsaw resources so that the passively uninvolved student has materials or information the others need. Either the student will share materials or group members will include the student in order to get the needed material.
- Assign tasks and be sure the passively uninvolved student takes a turn at each one — reader, writer, etc.
- Offer a reward based on individual performance which will motivate the passively uninvolved individual, or the group, to become involved.

Active Uninvolvement

Typical Behaviors:

- Talking about everything but the task
- Leaving the group without the group's permission
- Attempting to sabotage the group's work by giving wrong answers or destroying the product
- Refusing to work with someone in the group

Suggested Strategy:

- Structure individual accountability by offering a reward that this individual or group finds attractive. Tie it to a test or checking system so the actively uninvolved person must cooperate in order for the group to succeed and get the reward.

Independence of Groupmates

Typical Behaviors:

- Uninvolvement with the group
- Doing work alone
- Ignoring group discussion

Suggested Strategies:

+ Jigsaw materials so that the independent student cannot do the work without obtaining materials from the other students. To accomplish the task, the individual must interact and cooperate.
+ Limit resources. If there is only one answer sheet and pencil, this person is unable to do the work alone.

Taking Charge of Groupmates

Typical Behaviors:

+ Doing all the work
+ Refusing to let others help
+ Ordering others around
+ Bullying group members
+ Making decisions without checking for agreement

Suggested Strategies:

+ Jigsaw resources so that this person must cooperate with others to obtain the needed materials or information.
+ Assign tasks so that everyone in the group has a turn to read, write, draw, etc., not just the take charge person.
+ Use individual accountability and rewards. If everyone has to take an individual test and meet criteria to get the reward, group members are likely to take their turns and not allow one individual to assume total responsibility for completing the task.

STUDENT WITH SEVERE BEHAVIOR OR EMOTIONAL PROBLEMS

We know that students with severe behavior or emotional problems can be difficult to deal with in the classroom. If you have one or more of these students, please note the suggestions above and implement those first. Be sure that you have given ample practice on social skills and group work; once or twice will not be enough. Resist giving up after only a few tries.

Make a friend of the special education consultant. Discover what each of your inclusion students is and is not capable of doing; i.e., cutting; self-control in small group; attention span, etc. With the special education expert and the student in question, set expectations for group behavior and schedule frequent check-in sessions to process behavior.

Remember that implementing cooperative learning does not mean throwing out your discipline program. If a student consistently breaks classroom and group guidelines AND you have carefully built in all of the critical attributes, then you may have to fall back on other consequences (time out, conference with teacher, removal from classroom, etc.)

We suggest that you closely examine your discipline program. Some procedures are more complementary to cooperative learning than others. You might want to consider two models, one called *Cooperative Discipline* by Linda Albert or another called *Positive Discipline* by Jane Nelsen (see resources). Both programs honor young people and provide ideas for thoughtful consequences.

Conclusion

No matter how formal or informal your cooperative groups are, it is essential to build in some form of positive interdependence and individual accountability. Experiment with the ones that seem easiest to implement, try out new ones as you continue to use cooperative learning. Be sure to notice what type of problems occur when students are working in groups and make decisions on which forms of positive interdependence and individual accountability could influence problem behaviors.

PLANNING YOUR FIRST 5-STEP LESSON

We created the 5-step cooperative learning lesson some years ago in response to teachers saying, "How can I build social skills practice into groups I'm already using?" We found that most teachers did not have the essential elements in place in the groups they were using, so teaching social skills seemed premature. Only when the foundation is in place, can students begin to consciously practice the skills that truly make groups work.

As you know from the 3-step cooperative learning lesson (Chapter 3), there are some behaviors that need to be included in any lesson. Following is an outline including two new steps and an expanded teacher's role.

THE 5-STEP COOPERATIVE LEARNING LESSON

I. Subject Matter Directions

> positive interdependence
> individual accountability
> face-to-face interaction

II. Assign Social Skill

> ask students for reasons to use
> brainstorm "sounds like" and "looks like" — write on chart paper

III. Teacher Monitors

> observes for social skill — uses observation form

IV. Process Social Skill

> individual → group → whole class → teacher

V. Process Subject Matter

> see products
> hear reports/responses
> correct work
> discuss academic skills

CHAPTER 5

Following is an explanation of the five steps and how they differ from the 3-step cooperative learning lesson.

Step I. Subject Matter Directions

This step refers to writing and posting directions for students that include positive interdependence and individual accountability (Chapter 4) and face-to-face interaction. The latter refers to the physical arrangement of chairs, desks, and tables to foster cooperation and positive interactions between students (Chapter 3).

Step II. Assign Social Skill

Pick one specific social skill for students to practice along with the subject matter. We offer a variety of social skills from which to choose and the criteria for determining which one to assign in Chapter 8. During this step, students are asked to consider reasons why this social skill is the one assigned, why the social skill is important and what it might look like and sound like as they work through their group assignment. These brainstormed possible behaviors are written on chart paper by the teacher so students can refer back to them as they work and after the group time is over.

Step III. Teacher Monitors

In the 5-step model, along with walking around silently noticing what students are doing with the content, the teacher fills in an observation form. This form is a record of behaviors students were seen and heard practicing when using the social skill. This helps focus the teacher on behaviors to be observed, as well as being a visual reminder for students that using social skill behaviors is expected and reinforced. (See Chapter 8 for more information.)

Step IV. Process Social Skill

Individuals react to a specific statement or sentence, discuss reactions within the group, then report out to the whole class. The teacher also gives feedback and offers brief comments. (See Chapter 9 for complete information.) This step is essential when including a social skill because without the discussion of how the social skill was used, could have been used more, and what to change or continue, students will neglect the social skill. If processing is used, students will also be more likely to transfer learnings from the group work to other parts of their lives.

Step V. Process Subject Matter

It is not enough to process only how students worked on social skills. It is also important to process how they did on the task. This includes checking the work itself, hearing some/all reports, and/or asking students to process their thinking.

5-STEP LESSON PLAN WORKSHEET

We created this lesson plan form to help you plan your lessons. It can reduce the anxieties you and your students might experience as you attempt both group work and a social skill (see Appendix B for a blank form). The rest of this chapter includes a description of decisions necessary to fill in this form. Obviously, once cooperative groups become an integral part of your teaching repertoire, you will no longer need to complete the worksheet for each 5-step cooperative learning lesson and will do so only if you want to be able to replicate the lesson or pass it on to someone else.

Read the explanation for each step of the model lesson plan; consider the examples from a sample lesson provided as well as the suggestions offered. You might want to make a copy of the 5-Step Lesson Plan Form in Appendix B and fill in the blanks with possibilities of what you could use. As you work through the steps outlined in this chapter, you will be creating your first 5-step cooperative learning lesson plan.

Step 1: Subject Matter Content

There are 5 parts to Step 1. The first part concerns choosing a lesson. We have two suggestions:

First, begin with an academic task. Often groups are used for meaningless or time-filler tasks. We want students to know that groups are appropriate for "real work" too. It is, however, important to structure team building activities in addition to academic tasks when beginning the use of cooperative learning. Team building helps students begin caring for groupmates even as they practice skills and concepts. (Chapter 3 and Appendix I contain ideas for team building.)

Second, use academic tasks and skills which are familiar to your students. The tasks listed in Appendix G, "Academic Tasks for Cooperative Groups," have been used successfully with groups who are novices in terms of 5-step lessons. These tasks require familiar skills and their successful completion has academic merit.

You increase the possibility that this first 5-step cooperative group activity will be successful if you choose an activity or procedure with which your students are familiar. This also allows students to concentrate on the new group behaviors and social skill you will be assigning them to practice.

Step 1-A. Learning Objective

Determine the objective of your lesson; that is, the information or skill you want students to acquire or practice.

1-A. Learning Objective: Information/Skill to be learned:

Current events information: practice communication skills

Step 1-B. Group Goal

When deciding on your first 5-step lesson group task, consider an amount of work that can be completed during one class session, including time for giving directions and processing. Be sure to clarify for students that this is a group task. Work is not to be done individually or competitively, but cooperatively.

1-B. Group Goal:

Each student is to share a current event; each person's event is listed on group paper; everyone is to listen and be ready to report on any groupmate's event.

Step 1-C. Name of Strategy (if applicable)

This refers to the list of strategies we include in Appendix H. If you choose to use one of those, write the title of it here.

1-C. Name of Strategy:

Show & Tell / Bring & Brag

Step 1-D. Learning Experience(s) that Precedes Group Work

The fourth part of Step 1 is to determine what learning experience(s) will precede group work. This could be a direct instruction lesson including some sort of review, video, demonstration, etc. Keep this part short for your first 5-step lessons, as the lesson will be lengthy already. It is also an option to cover new material the day before; then, with a brief review, launch into the 5-step lesson.

1-D. Learning Experience(s) that precedes group work

Check over homework from each student; group makes sure that each student has a current event to share.

Step 1-E. Length of Work Time

The fifth and final part of Step 1 is to plan how much time students will have to work in their groups. We believe that this needs to be a specific amount of time, as many students tend to be leisurely about getting started if they do not understand that time is limited. We recommend work time between 10-25 minutes, depending on the age and experience of students, type of activity, etc. Ten minutes is a minimum amount of time to get around to all of the groups during work time. We also find that 30 minutes is a maximum amount of time for any group to work without a chance to check-in, process, discuss how the work is going. This applies to learners of all ages, experience, or type of activity.

1-E. Length of Work Time: *10 minutes*

Step 2: Group Composition and Room Arrangement

How many students in a group, who is in which group, and how your room is arranged are all important management items to decide before group work begins. (See Chapter 3.) These decisions fall into several categories.

Step 2-A. Group Size

Begin with the size of your groups. Our recommendation is to start with groups of 3 for a 5-step lesson. We recommend 3 because groups larger than 3 require more time for work and processing. The uneven number of three encourages discussion and questioning and yet is small enough to get the task done in a reasonable amount of time.

2A. Group Size: *3 or 4*

Step 2-B. Assignment to Groups

Decide how you will choose who works in which groups. Refer to Chapter 3 for the choices we recommend. This process needs to be done thoughtfully and consciously, as it has important ramifications for group work.

2B. Assignment to Groups: (choose one)

☒   Random Method: *Pick names from "Winner's Basket"*

☐   Teacher-selected Criteria: _____   _____

Step 2C. Duration of Group

Another consideration is how long this group will stay together. It could be just for this lesson and no other, for the length of a unit of study, the semester, or the school year. There is no one right answer for this. We recommend setting the duration ahead of time, so students will know how long they will be together. We also recommend that students work in more than one group, so that there are short-term groups going on, as well as one home-base, on-going group. This makes it reasonable to change neighbors for "Turn to Your Neighbor" every week, be in a new group for a 3 week unit, as well as feel the safety, security, and bonding of a home-base group.

2C. Duration of Group: marking period — *10 weeks*

Step 2D. Room Arrangement

Desk and room arrangement are important factors in group productivity and in maintaining your sanity. As we covered in Chapter 3, the scraping of thirty desks across the room will not endear you to your colleagues and will not help strengthen your belief that groups are a pleasant part of your instructional repertoire. Deciding how you want the room to look when students are working in cooperative groups and how you will achieve that look are preplanning *musts*. Reread the considerations in Chapter 3, then decide on Step 2D.

2D. Room Arrangement: *Students sit in a circle of 3 or 4 chairs.*

Step 3: Positive Interdependence

As we covered in Chapter 4, you need to build in positive interdependence since not all students will automatically want to work with others in a cooperative group. Therefore, we need to create a feeling of "We sink or swim together."

We offer you five options and ask that you consider each carefully for your first 5-step lesson plan.

Step 3-A. Materials

The materials given to students can be limited or jigsawed. Sharing limited materials, such as one paper and one pencil, helps group members draw together to complete an assignment. Limiting resources is important not only in light of budget constraints, but also as an effective way to increase the chances that cooperation will occur within the group.

To jigsaw materials means that everyone in the group gets a part of the necessary materials and the group needs all of the parts to complete the group task.

At this point, you also need to decide how many materials you need per student or group and what they are.

3A. Materials

		# Needed	Description
☒	Limited	*1*	*answer sheet to outline each others' events*
		1	*clipboard*
☒	Jigsawed	*1*	*current event for each student*

Step 3-B. One Product

What product, if any, will students create? Will it be a group answer sheet, list, picture, collage, paragraph? It is helpful at this point for students to actually create a product as this gives them something concrete on which to focus. In this lesson each student takes a turn writing a brief description of someone else's current event. The result is a description of each event. This activity helps everyone focus on each contribution.

3B. One product: *group answer sheet*

Step 3-C. Common Goal

In some cooperative learning activities in which students do not create a product, it is essential to build in a common goal. It is important when a product is created as well, especially when students are to be held accountable for the information gathered by other groupmates.

    ☒ **3B. Common Goal:** *All group members are to be sure that everyone in group writes on group form and can report on any other member's current event.*

Step 3-D. Rotate Roles

As we listed in Chapter 3, we recommend roles that refer more to mechanics than status: reader, writer, messenger, drawer, proofreader, etc. Each person is to take a turn during group work time to perform the roles assigned.

    ☒ **3-D. Rotate roles:** *writer*

Step 3-E. Reward

This is the time to decide whether or not rewards are required to help motivate students to stay on task and/or help groupmates be successful. If you decide after reviewing the section on rewards in Chapter 4 (*Positive Interdependence and Individual Accountability*) that this is necessary, please choose one reward and fill in the following blanks. (Note that we have chosen no reward for this lesson because we believe in the use of rewards only when all else has failed!) Also fill out how students can earn the reward (criteria for receiving) and be sure to have a reason to use one.

    ☒ **3-E. Reward:** *none*   Criteria for receiving: _____

Reason to use: _____

Step 4: Individual Accountability

This area, too, was covered thoroughly in Chapter 4. To refresh your memory, choose a way to let students know that you will be checking on individuals after group work to determine the depth of participation, understanding and/or mastery. It is possible to choose all three methods, especially if your students are resistant to working together.

☒ **4A. Signatures** (on front): *All sign group answer sheet*

☒ **4B. Random Check (explain method):** *Pick names from "Winner's Basket" to tell groupmates current event (groupmate chosen by teacher).*

❑ **4C. Individual performance** (explain): *none*

Step 5: Subject Matter Directions

In this section, you write out the directions you will actually give to students. These will be written up, either on an easel, paper taped to the chalkboard, or overhead projector transparency. (There is a place to check one of these in Step 5.) Students then have the directions to refer to during work time instead of having to call you over, becoming creative about what to do next, or getting off task because no one can agree about what they are to do. Note also that the amount of work time students will have (Step 1E) is written out for students here.

Step 5: Subject Matter Directions: State in language your students will understand.

"Your group will work cooperatively to:

1. *Listen to each other's current event.*

2. *Each person writes down most important points of someone else's current event on group paper.*

3. *Be ready to report on any of the other reports.*

4. *Be sure that everyone in your group is ready to report."*

10 minutes work time

Where to display for students:

❏ easel   ❏ chalkboard   ☒ screen

Step 6: Social Skill

As we carefully detail in Chapter 8, you choose one social skill to assign to students based on their past performance, age, task to be done, etc. (Please read over that chapter for choices as well as rationale.) In this lesson, the teacher chose to assign the task skill of "Check for Understanding" because students often act as if they comprehend what others are talking about, but when they are asked to report are often at a loss as to what was actually said.

There is also a spot on Step 6 of the lesson plan form to choose what type of observation form will be used (also outlined in Chapter 8). This teacher decided to use the multi-group form, since with 34 students she had 11 groups to observe! This meant that she had only two sheets to handle and that she could stand in one place and observe several groups at one time.

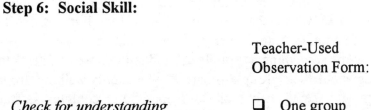

Step 6: Social Skill:

Teacher-Used
Observation Form:

Check for understanding   ❏ One group

☒ Multi-group

❏ Classroom

Step 7: Process Social Skill

Chapter 9 is devoted to how processing social skills can be done in a 5-step lesson. We recommend that you choose one of the 3 statements listed on the form as a beginning processing statement. This teacher chose the statement marked in this lesson because her students looked most often for what went wrong rather than on what they did well.

The statement is written on the board, transparency, or on the group paper for students to respond to in writing (if they have enough skills) or they may respond orally.

Step 7: Process Social Skill (after work time):

(Choose one statement for students to complete)

☒ We did well on _*checking for understanding*_ by _____, _____, and _____.
(3 specific behaviors)

❏ I liked the way I helped my group today by _____.

❏ In any group it is helpful to _____ because
(social skill)
_____.

Step 8: Process Subject Matter

This is the point where students get closure on the cooperative learning lesson in which they have been involved. Even if the lesson carries over to another time or day, it is important to process the subject matter. It may be something as simple as randomly chosen students telling a few words about their group's progress, or students walking around to other groups and seeing their projects. It may be as complex as students hearing reports from each group and taking their own notes so they will be ready for an individual quiz on the material.

Notice that processing the subject matter comes after processing the social skill. We have noticed that if students get closure on the task, it is difficult to get them to focus on the social skill. Also, especially in the beginning stages, it is more important to process the social skill immediately than the subject matter, since that can be done later in the day or during the next class period.

For this lesson, the teacher decided to hear a few responses by calling on students from the Winner's Basket.

Step 8: Process Subject Matter (after work time)

☒ Hear responses (all or some)

☐ See products (all or some)

☐ Students check products

☒ Hand in products

☐ Discussion of academic skills

Summary

These initial decisions may seem time consuming because they are! You will find, though, that they will facilitate the implementation of your first 5-step cooperative learning lesson. Now that these decisions are made, the steps outlined in Chapter 6 will further help you put your plan into action.

5-STEP LESSON PLAN IMPLEMENTATION

Students: "Where is Group 3? I can't find my group."

"You want me to work with *her?* No way!"

"Now what are we supposed to do?"

Teacher: "Okay, students, quiet down. Why is there so much commotion in your groups?"

Even the best plans can fail unless you consciously decide how to put your lesson plan into action. Careful pre-planning *plus* careful implementation increases the possibility of positive group experiences for you and your students. Our suggestions come with no guarantee, but many teachers find that implementing these steps increases the likelihood that group work will be effective and satisfying for you and your students.

We suggest that you read this chapter as you would a road map. You may want to follow it step-by-step for your first experience as a cooperative group facilitator of a 5-step lesson. Notice that the presentation to students is in a slightly different order than the lesson plan outlined in Chapter 5. Explanations are arranged chronologically, according to whether they are given before, during, or after group work.

Please read or reread Chapter 3 if you haven't recently read it. There we cover many ways to give students a "mindset" for cooperation.

YOUR FIRST 5-STEP LESSON

Before Group Work

The first step in implementation is to complete any learning experience(s) that precedes group work (Step 1-D). Conduct the direct instruction lesson, review, demonstration, etc.

CHAPTER 6

At this point you may be tempted to put students into groups and then give them directions. Consider this question first. What happens as soon as students get into groups? Of course, *they talk*. Sometimes their talk is about the assignment; sometimes it is about totally unrelated topics. Generally, it is most effective to give all directions before students move into groups.

Subject Matter Directions (Step 5). Direct students' attention to the easel, chalkboard, or screen where you have posted the directions that you wrote for Step 5. We recommend uncovering each step one at a time (the "reveal" method) so that you have more control of student attention. Posting these directions sends the message, "This is important work." It also helps students answer the question, "What do we do next?"

Read the directions aloud and briefly explain that this is a cooperative activity. Students will not work alone or compete with classmates. Tell what materials go to each group and where they are located. At the beginning, you may choose to take materials around to each group so that they take *nothing* with them: no books, papers, pencils, crayons, etc. This helps them grasp that any materials they receive belong to the group, not just one person. If you prefer to designate one person in the group to be messenger (the only person who leaves the group to get materials from a central location), announce who it will be or remind students to choose someone. If you do not want to make this a formal role, tell students that only one person may leave to get materials and observe how students decide who leaves the group when it's necessary to do so.

Be sure it is clear to students how they will be checked after group work for individual accountability (Step 4). If you have decided to offer a reward, tell students what the reward will be and how and when each group member may obtain the reward (Step 3-E). Sometimes teachers do not tell students about individual accountability and rewards until after the group work has been completed. Afterwards is too late. These may be the components of the activity that help motivate students to become actively involved in the group. Do not keep them a secret.

Social Skills (Step 6). It is not enough to tell students the social skill and write it on the board or easel. (Since we recommend that you save the behaviors that students will brainstorm for this step, you will want to consider using an easel with paper or paper taped to the chalkboard.) Discuss why this social skill is important to use for this activity. Then add "sounds like" and "looks like" examples collected from the students to the chart paper. (See Chapter 8 for a detailed outline of this procedure.)

Teacher's Role. Tell students that your job during work time is to observe. Tell them what you will be observing for, why, what the observation form you will be using looks like, and how the information you collect will be used. Tell them that you are "invisible" unless they have *group* questions, and that you are not at each group to be an active member or to solve problems. (See Chapter 7 on Teacher's Role for specifics.)

Assignment to Groups (Step 2-B). If you chose in the 5-step lesson plan in Chapter 5 to select group members yourself, announce who is in which group. It is helpful to have student names written up if they need a reminder. If you are using a random method, you may also want to post names or have each group of students find one another and be seated before you go on to the next group.

Room Arrangement (Step 2-D). Arranging the room the way you planned may go well or it may look and sound like the world at war. To avoid confusion, you may want to:

- Arrange the room before students come into the room (before school or at lunch time).
- Give specific location directions to groups ("Group 1, sit here by my desk; Group 2, sit by the book shelf; Group 3, sit by the closet," etc.).
- Write or draw a diagram for students to follow.
- Have students practice how to get up and move quietly. (This is for students of *any* age!)
- Remind students that they need only to move themselves, not the furniture if you have prearranged the desks.
- Request that students do not take their own chairs; there will be one in the part of the room in which they will be meeting.

Remember that students will probably be less likely to want to get close to groupmates at the beginning of group work. The acronym "EEKK!" for eye-to-eye, knee-to-knee fits because many students say that when you tell them to get close in their groups. It is helpful, and often essential in some classrooms, to be sure that students understand why you are focusing them on being close. You might want to ask students why they think you are insisting on close proximity. It is not necessary for them to agree with your reasons, just be sure that they understand them.

It can also help create the "our classroom" feeling if students are involved in the decisions about how the room could be arranged to facilitate everyone being able to see and hear in their groups. If you do this, have students brainstorm possibilities (you might want to use the strategies "Pairs of Pairs" or "Advanced Pairs of Pairs" in Appendix H), choose one to try, then after implementation process how well it worked, what could be changed, etc.

Next, give the signal to move to groups. Some teachers use the word "Go!" with a visible start to the stop watch. Others say "You may begin." Without a definite beginning, the work will get off to a slow start, making it more difficult for students to get themselves organized and on task.

During Group Work

Place yourself away from the materials center or stay clear of the movement that is going on while students are getting themselves arranged. It is tempting to move things around for them, give orders, make suggestions, etc. Stay out of the way as students learn how to get things organized and begin. If there are problems or it goes remarkably smoothly, this can be noted in the processing after group work.

As groups begin working, go to the ones that are getting settled to begin recording your observations. Then work your way around the room, making notes of the exact words you see and hear. Be especially alert for non-verbal behaviors, such as gestures, eye contact, body position, proximity, etc. Observe and collect what you can; you will not be able to see and record everything.

You may have difficulty remembering to be invisible during group work time. You are not to make eye contact, laugh, frown, etc. Interrupting is always a judgment call and necessary at times if there is a serious problem. (See Chapter 7 for more information about guidelines for intervening in groups.) When there is a question, be sure to ask "Is this a group question?" before you call on one student to ask the group's question.

After Group Work

If you are holding students accountable by giving a test on information studied, give it at this time. Then you are ready to process social skills.

If you are not testing, move right to processing social skills, even if all groups are not finished with the work. Stop what is going on and give directions.

Write the processing statement on the board or have it on the overhead. Read aloud to students. They then discuss their reactions within their groups and at the end of this time (only 2-3 minutes), one person reports out any responses and/or new positive behaviors to add to the chart paper. The teacher can add these at this time, collect and add later, or have a group responsible for adding new ones.

At this point it is time to hand out observation forms. It is crucial NOT to hand out observation forms before this time, as students will not think about their own responses, but will only parrot what you have given them. Give students a minute or so to look over what you have written, or you, or students helpers, may go around to each group of non-readers and help them read what you collected. Students then discuss how the data you have collected are similar to and/or different from their perceptions. One person reports to the whole class any learnings. This is also a time when new positive behaviors can be added to the chart paper (or collected to be posted later). You will be tempted to skip this part and not have the reports from students. Consider that many students listen more to their peers than to you, so the value of students hearing from other students what they did that was positive in the group today can be immense. It is not just one more adult telling students how they ''should'' behave!

By this time in processing, most teachers would have given their opinions about how groups worked or didn't, what needs to be changed for next time, etc. We invite you to consider holding back your opinions until this point of processing and then making only one or two BRIEF comments about helpful and unhelpful behaviors you noticed. Realize that if there were major problems, you would have intervened and worked with that group during work time, so only make points about general sorts of things, especially if you can be descriptive rather than evaluative. Direct your comments to the whole class rather than specific groups or individuals, as this focuses attention on people and personalities, rather than on the behaviors. This is NOT a competition, rather a chance for students to hear what was seen and heard that the teacher considers to be appropriate and what was not. Being brief may be a struggle AND we believe that it is better to err on the side of too little. Students are used to hearing your opinions and more of the same will only keep them from thinking on their own and deciding what to continue and what to improve.

Now that processing of social skills is done, it is time to process the subject matter. You can correct group work, if appropriate and necessary at this time; hear reports or responses from some or all groups; see group products; discuss academic skills.

At this point, it is time for students to sign the group paper if they haven't done so already, put the observation form and unfinished work in the group folder (since the group paper should NEVER leave the room if you ever want to see it again!), and do a general clean-up, putting materials and furniture back.

After Class is Over

We recommend that you process the lesson yourself the same day (if you are unable to do so immediately after the lesson) by writing out what you liked most, what you liked least, and what you want to change in your next cooperative learning lesson. Some teachers do this in their plan books, some in a journal. We recommend setting a timer for 2-3 minutes so that you do this consistently. The most important thing is doing it EVERY time you do group work, rather than once in a while. If you process for 20 minutes once, you will be unlikely to do it again because it's rare for most of us to free up 20 minutes in a row for anything! Only by consciously processing what has occurred will you support your own growth and learning so that this process becomes habitual and comfortable.

THE TEACHER'S ROLE
DURING GROUP WORK

The stage is now set for your first cooperative group lesson.

Your lesson plan is complete, the materials are assembled, and the students are seated in their groups. You have skillfully led students through the directions and have posted them for students to see. Your students know that you will be busy monitoring group work. They also know that you expect them to depend on themselves and their groupmates to answer questions or solve problems that might arise.

With hopes high for a successful experience, you watch as students begin to work. You place yourself near a group, prepared to observe students so closely that you will not miss a nuance of any skill. The threesome you are observing is arguing over who is going to write first. You glance up at the sound of angry words and see two students engaged in a shouting match in a nearby group. You suddenly notice hands up in a group across the room. As you consider what to do next, a student approaches and asks, "Can I sharpen my pencil?"

What to do now? How can you concentrate on your task of observing when there are other distractions and demands? How you deal with these questions and behaviors during this first cooperative group experience is critical. What you do will determine how well students learn to solve their own problems, how often they demand your attention in the future, and whether or not you attempt to do groups again! What you need right now is not a lesson plan, not tips on how to arrange desks, not ideas for building in individual accountability. What you need is an action plan for dealing with these demands from students. Creating that action plan is the focus for the rest of this chapter.

To begin your plan, you need to decide what type of responses you want to make to students. Let's examine two sets of beliefs that affect how you respond. One involves your beliefs about students making mistakes during work time, and the other concerns the teacher's role in solving students' problems.

TEACHER REACTIONS TO STUDENT MISTAKES

The first step is to define the work "mistake." Webster's definition is "a wrong action or statement proceeding from faulty judgment, inadequate knowledge, or inattention." We like to add the following phrase to this definition: "...that indicates that more practice is needed and more skill lessons are necessary before mastery occurs."

If your belief is that making mistakes shows that students have not yet learned all the necessary skills, you probably look at mistakes as data. When students make mistakes working in groups, you continue to give them chances to practice as well as teach additional lessons on social skills.

If, on the other hand, you believe that mistakes show that students are unwilling or unable to do the task, you are likely to refuse to let students work in groups unless they do it perfectly every time. Since students will not do it perfectly every time because they have not learned the skills, you will probably abandon the use of group work.

Notice that this latter reaction to mistakes made during group work by students is very different from teacher reaction to errors made in subject matter areas. Have you ever heard a teacher say to students, "OK, that's it! No more math for you kids. I'm sick and tired of your mistakes. When you show me that you can do math, then I'll give you some and not until!"? As teachers we realize the need for mistakes in the process of learning any new skill. If students are not making mistakes in math, or spelling, or reading they are not learning anything because they have already learned it. If they never miscalculate, misspell, or misread, we know they have mastered the skill and it is time to move on to a new skill. This means more mistakes and new learning. When it comes to learning skills for cooperative groups, there is really no difference in the learning process.

THE TEACHER'S ROLE IN
SOLVING STUDENT PROBLEMS

Let's consider one of the goals of cooperative learning: to create independent learners. If we trust that students can get along without us, we have to model that belief in our behavior during group work time. We do not leave them alone, rather we give each student a group for support.

As pointed out in Chapter 2, one of the differences between cooperative groups and typical classroom groups is that in cooperative groups teachers use interacting behaviors when students have problems in groups. When students have problems during individual work time, we respond to and help individuals. When students are in groups, we want to respond to the group by only answering group questions. When students are in groups, we give them the time and space to rely on their own skills and thinking. This is not because responding to individuals or prompting groups is wrong and staying out of groups is right, but because there are very different outcomes for student depending on which helping behaviors you tend to use.

If you believe that students need you to solve their problems, chances are that your tendency is to intervene. Teachers use intervening behaviors when they hover over groups (we call that "helicoptering"), break into groups to settle arguments (whether or not they are asked for help), tell students what to do, remind, threaten, give advice, or praise. The belief is that without teacher intervention to motivate and remind, students will not be successful. If you believe that students are capable of solving their own problems, you are more likely to interact with groups. Teachers who use interacting behaviors remain "invisible" and interrupt only when asked by students for help, or when there is an emergency. They resist praising students during work time. Instead they give feedback about positive and negative behaviors during processing. (See Chapter 9.)

OUTCOMES FOR INTERVENING
OR INTERACTING BEHAVIORS

There are short- and long-term outcomes for both intervening and interacting behaviors. By looking at these outcomes you will be able to decide which types of behavior you want to use more often when students are working in groups.

Intervening Behaviors

The short-term outcomes of intervening to remind students of expected behaviors sound desirable: students return to the task; complete the work; and accomplish their goal. They stop inappropriate behavior or feel good about the praise bestowed upon them by the teacher. The long-term outcomes seem less attractive. Students become dependent on the teacher to convince them to keep busy and use social skills. Because it is the teacher's prodding that keeps things rolling, there is little ownership by the group for their success or failure. Also, groups avoid experiencing the consequences of not working out their difficulties independently, since they know that the teacher will bail them out if they have problems.

Interacting Behaviors

The short-term outcomes of interacting with students are not always pleasant. Without the teacher's intervening, students often spend time in conflict, at first. As a result, the work is often not completed, so the group is not "successful." The long-term payoffs, however, are worth the discomfort of using interacting behaviors during your first cooperative group experiences. When students learn to work things out for themselves, they get to work quickly without relying on the teacher's reminders. They stay on task and ask for help on appropriate occasions. They experience a sense of ownership for their success or failure as a group and are more likely to put forth the energy to continue to solve problems when they occur. Handling such situations helps students develop a feeling of power and potency.

Obviously, it is up to you to decide which set of outcomes you prefer. If you do not mind students continually looking to you to rescue them or if you require, at all costs, that the assigned work be completed, intervening will be your dominant mode. Just be aware of the probable outcomes so that you are not surprised when students seem to constantly need your help and approval.

It is important to decide *ahead of time* which behaviors you would like to use. Do you prefer to use more intervening or interacting behaviors? Do not wait until the questions come, the arguments start, or the loner is ignored. Make that decision now and be conscious of your intentions.

Types of Situations Requiring Teacher Input

There are two types of situations which may occur during work time which require a response from you even if that response is to ignore inappropriate behaviors. One type of situation is when students are having difficulty and ask you for help. Their questions sometimes deal with subject matter and sometimes with social skills. If you choose intervening behaviors, you will answer every question and respond to every comment made to you. If students ask how to spell a word, you will tell them. If they want to know what the directions are, you will repeat them. If there are complaints about group members, you will listen and solve the problem; this might include behaviors ranging from persuading students to cooperate to breaking up the group. If you choose to use interacting behaviors, you will ignore comments and questions directed at you and will only respond to "group" questions. These are questions which everyone in the group is prepared to ask, since everyone discussed possible answers. When the teacher is signaled by the group, the teacher chooses one student to ask the question. Then s/he turns it back to them by asking, "What does your group think?" or "What have you tried so far?" In this way you will discover whether the group needs an academic skill reviewed, such as alphabetical order; or if they need help thinking of ways to solve a social skill problem, such as how to include a groupmate in the group's work.

The other type of situation is when students are obviously having some difficulty and they do *not* ask you for help. If you choose to use intervening behaviors, you will interrupt the group and tell them what to do, issue threats, give reminders, cajole with praise, or deliver a lecture. This, as we have already explained, will usually take care of the problem in the short run, although you might have to return to dispense another dose of intervention later.

If you choose to use interacting behaviors, you will generally choose to let students deal with the problem(s) themselves. They will either settle the difficulty themselves, ask you for help, or become so disruptive that you may decide to break into the group. We recommend keeping your interruptions to a minimum. Break in only for what you think are serious situations. If you do interrupt at this point, use interacting behaviors to return the problem to the group for a solution. You may wish to employ the following procedure:

1) Describe the behavior that you observe.

2) Ask what the group has done so far to solve the problem.

3) Ask what they are going to do next.

4) Support the group as they brainstorm several solutions if they have no alternatives.

5) Let the group choose a solution to implement.

6) Come back to check on how well the solution is working. (See Chapter 2 for a description of how interacting problem-solving worked in Mr. Jordan's classroom.)

It may require checking back with the group several times, but turning problems back to the group to solve will result in long-term independent, problem-solving behavior being used by groups.

TEST YOUR COMFORT ZONE

Whether you do mainly intervening or interacting behaviors, we encourage you to risk moving from the ones you are using now to ones that are more interactive. This does not mean that you ignore every request for help and insist that students solve *all* of their own problems. It does mean that you behave in ways which are more interactive than your usual style. If you generally intervene, decide in what situations you will only interact. Also decide under what circumstances you will intervene. If that occasion does arise, wait a few seconds longer than you normally would, just to stretch yourself and give students a little more time to resolve the problem themselves. Decide on a strategy beforehand so that you will not be as likely to slip back to former behaviors during a classroom crisis.

ACTION PLAN

Now that you have decided which behaviors you would like to use more often, put together an action plan for yourself.

Inform Students

No matter what you decide about your behavior, let students know ahead of time what you will be doing. Inform students that you will only answer group questions. Tell them how they can get your attention as well as how you will know it's really a group question. This will save you time, energy, and shoe leather later.

Do What You Announce

Do not announce that you will be "invisible" during observation time and then react to students whenever they say anything to you. If you say you are invisible, do not respond to eye contact, talk to students, or interact in any way.

Look for Measures of Success

Decide on one or two small measures of success so that you can maintain motivation for future interacting behaviors. Some measures of success might be that fewer students come up to you when you are observing, or that more of them ignore you when you are observing their groups, or that no one in a group acts differently when you appear. Determine two or three specific observable behaviors which will help you know that your new behaviors are beginning to have an impact.

Process Your New Behaviors

After each cooperative group, notice which of your behaviors you liked and want to continue. Be gentle with yourself. By concentrating on the behavior, rather than bemoaning the things you wish you had done differently, you will make faster progress and enjoy the journey more!

Set Goals for Yourself

After each session, set one specific goal for what you will continue to do or what you will do differently during the next cooperative group lesson. Keep the wording positive. A goal of "I will let students keep track of time" is more helpful than "I will not give students a two minute warning."

We encourage you to examine your beliefs and behaviors in order to develop your action plan. Writing it out is most helpful, but just considering it is also beneficial. You will find it is worth the thought and effort to be prepared for on the spot student demands.

You have decided which of the helping behaviors you plan to use with students and how you are going to put your plan into action. Now it is time to look at some specific ways to help students practice social skills and process their use of those skills. Section III of this book will help you move "Beyond the Basics."

TEACHING
SOCIAL SKILLS

Does this sound too good to be true? Have you finally lucked out if you hear kids say:

"I don't get it, Jane."
"That's okay, Tom. I'll explain it another way."
"Thanks for that idea, Sue. I never thought of it that way before."
"No, Steve, I don't agree with that answer. Show me how you figured problem 16."

No, you're not dreaming. These are words that have been said by students in cooperative groups. Although you probably did not hear such skilled responses in your first group lesson, they do occur, but not by accident.

Over and over again, teachers have asked students to work on an assignment in groups, with added directions of "Get along," or "Cooperate." You have said that to students; we have too. But we all know that such statements are not sufficient. Students need to learn the skills of cooperation right from scratch, just as they need to learn to read or to follow directions. We need to teach them those cooperative skills, step by step. In this chapter we will:

- ◆ Look at what social skills are and why they are necessary.
- ◆ Consider which skills to use when beginning 5-step cooperative learning lessons and how to progress in the use of social skills.
- ◆ Outline the steps that are necessary to teach social skills as well as the procedure for observing how students use them.
- ◆ Take a glimpse at how to phase out the assignment of social skills.

CHAPTER 8

RETHINKING LEADERSHIP

Leadership looks and sounds different in cooperative groups than in typical classroom groups. It will be helpful if you and your students examine old definitions of leadership and establish new pictures from which to work.

Student leaders abound in schools. Some class leaders exhibit positive characteristics when they:

- Volunteer for duties.

- Initiate pro-social activities.

- Maintain positive attitudes towards teachers, peers, and school.

- Enter fully into school life.

These leaders are often the academic achievers, the class officers, and the athletes who are team members.

Other student leaders exhibit negative characteristics when they:

- Exhibit isolation, alone or in an antisocial gang.

- Decline or ignore positive activities.

- Initiate misbehavior.

- Scorn everyday school life.

These are the leaders that educators often try to ignore, hope will outgrow their behavior, or pass on to the next grade.

In classrooms, teachers often use the positive leaders to advance academic goals by selecting them to oversee class activities, especially in group work. One of two things is likely to happen:

- The chosen leader succeeds in organizing the group into some semblance of a productive unit.

- The chosen leader ends up doing all the work for the group, resenting being put-upon and is disliked by the group for being productive.

The negative leaders are often ignored, dispersed among groups with the hope that they will not spoil projects, or corralled into a group where they sabotage only themselves. Their influence is seen as an irritation to normal classroom procedures.

Neither type of leader was born with those characteristics, nor were they handed their behaviors along with the roles they have learned to play. Both positive and negative student leaders learn to repeat and refine their behaviors, consciously or subconsciously, as they receive the rewards of attention and reinforcement from adults and their peers. Since both sorts of leaders have status with their peers, this leadership power can be channeled by teachers to positive advantage.

Leadership in cooperative groups involves the use of social skills by all group members. By practicing social skills:

- Positive leaders learn to share their responsibilities.
- Negative leaders learn to channel their behaviors into useful activities while still receiving attention from peers and adults.
- Followers learn the skills of positive leadership thereby receiving both extrinsic and intrinsic rewards.

Every member can win in cooperative groups. We will now look at the skills required to improve every student's leadership.

A DEFINITION OF SOCIAL SKILLS

Social skills are those specific behaviors performed by all group members which help the group complete the task and appreciate each other when the task is finished. David and Roger Johnson have categorized social skills as either "task" or "maintenance" skills. Both types must be practiced consistently if the group is to maintain itself as a positive, effective unit.

Task Skills

In the process of achieving a specific objective, there are many discrete behaviors involved. Task skills have a content focus and are necessary whether the job is to make a list, draw a picture, memorize facts, complete a project, or answer a sheet of questions.

Examples of task social skills are:

- Contribute ideas
- Keep track of time
- Follow directions

If group members do not perform task skills, the group can founder and fail to meet its subject matter objective. The consistent use of these skills helps the group work effectively to create a high-quality product or outcome.

Maintenance Skills

In order for the group to continue working effectively together, it is not sufficient to complete the task. There must also be an emphasis on the contributions of each individual group member. Such emphasis builds group cohesiveness and stability.

We have already introduced the skill "Respond to Ideas Respectfully." Other maintenance skills are:

- Check for agreement
- One person talks at a time
- Encourage

Use of these skills helps students feel better about themselves, each other, and the group. Without these behaviors, a group single-mindedly completes the task with little acknowledgment of the individuals involved. Without such caring, groups rarely enjoy the process or want to continue meeting on a regular basis.

Both task and maintenance skills are necessary for groups to work effectively. If a group completes the task, but none of the members ever wants to see or work with the others again, that is not a successful cooperative group. If, on the other hand, a group has a wonderful time and everyone feels cared for and respected but the task was not started, that is not a successful cooperative group either. The goal of teaching social skills is the creation of groups which consist of positive, on-task students who show respect for each other.

There are many social skills that you may introduce to your students. We have suggestions to assist you when choosing beginning skills as well as a list of skills from which to choose for future cooperative group experiences.

Beginning Social Skills

The first social skills chosen for cooperative groups must do two things:

- Provide students with practice of the skills needed to do the assigned work.
- Provide students with practice of the skills needed to work together in a positive manner.

In light of these considerations, we recommend that you choose from four fundamental social skills:

- **Task Skills**

    Check for understanding
    Share ideas

- **Maintenance Skills**

    Encourage
    Check for agreement

These skills provide the initial task and maintenance motivation required to get a cooperative group started. They provide a foundation of social skills upon which groups will be able to build cooperation.

There are also more advanced skills you may introduce to your students. A list of typical social skills that successful group members use follows:

SOCIAL SKILLS

Task Skills

Lower Elementary	**Upper El/M.S.**	**H.S./Adult**
Check for understanding	Check for understanding	Check for understanding
Share ideas	Contribute ideas	Contribute ideas
Get group back to work	Get group back to work	Get group back to work
Ask questions	Ask questions	Seek information and opinions
Follow directions	Follow directions	Follow directions
Keep track of time	Keep track of time	Keep track of time

Maintenance Skills

Lower Elementary	**Upper El/M.S.**	**H.S./Adult**
Check for agreement	Check for agreement	Check for agreement
Encourage	Encourage	Encourage
Invite others to talk	Encourage others to talk	Encourage others to talk
Answer back politely	Respond to ideas respectfully	Respond to ideas respectfully
One person talks at a time	One person talks at a time	One person talks at a time
Disagree in a nice way	Disagree in an agreeable way	Disagree in an agreeable way

As you can see from the three columns, the skills necessary to work in groups are the same from preschool through graduate school. It is only the vocabulary that may change. Choose the words that best fit your students regardless of the columns to which they refer. For example, some junior high students prefer to call encouraging behaviors "cheerleading" since that is a role with which they are familiar.

Notice that these lists do not contain the words "cooperation," "respect," or "listening." We believe that these are goals, not individual skills. They are outcomes of using many social skills successfully. When we assign "respond to ideas respectfully," for example, we are leading students toward respect and cooperation.

Although this list may look complete, it is not. Please notice the blank after each column. This indicates that there are many more social skills than the ones listed here. Social skills arise from need — what the group perceives it needs to operate more effectively as well as what the teacher perceives the group needs. If a group is having trouble because group members are not talking about the work, it is time to have "Get group back to work" as a social skill. If some group members are having trouble coming up with ideas, then "Contribute ideas" becomes a helpful social skill to practice. If students are all talking at once, then a possible social skill would be "One person talks at a time."

At this point, we would like to offer a gentle reminder. While you want your students to use all of these and other social skills as well, it is not reasonable to expect mastery of all of them in any given school year. We suggest that you pick several skills that are important to you in your particular classroom setting. Introduce those to your students, based on their proficiency in the area of cooperation.

Introducing and teaching social skills are not your only jobs as a cooperative group facilitator. In the beginning it is also necessary that you observe groups practicing social skills. We will now look at how you do that.

INTRODUCING A SOCIAL SKILL

It is not enough to tell students the social skill and write it on the board. It is necessary to introduce social skills to students before you ask them to practice those social skills, just as you introduce problem solving skills to students before you ask them to practice those skills on their own.

Spending time adequately preparing students to use social skills is time well spent. It is only necessary to do this introductory step once for each new skill, not each time the class does group work.

Tell students the title of the social skill. Ask students questions to stimulate a discussion:

"What does this mean to you?"

"How do you feel when people use it/don't use it when working with you?"

"Was this skill used by people in our recent story or current event?" (whole language or content connected)

After students have clarified why they are practicing this social skill, have them tell the specific behaviors that could be seen and heard as the skill is used. If you choose the social skill "Encourage," for example, write "Encourage" on chart paper. Then write the students' responses to the question "What does 'Encourage' sound like and look like?"

Encourage	
Sounds Like	Looks Like
"Way to go."	Smile
"Keep after it. You're almost there."	Pat on back
"Good job!"	Nod
"Let's try it again."	Leaning toward person

These are samples of how specific the behaviors must be in order to be effective and observable. We find that a minimum of three specific behaviors for each social skill is the most helpful. Notice, too, that we have included non-verbal as well as verbal behaviors, since messages are also sent through body language.

We suggest avoiding lists such as "What Not to Do in Groups" or "Bad Things for Group Members to Do." Putting these on display puts negative pictures in students' minds, rather than the positive images of what they are supposed to do to be helpful group members. It may be appropriate to discuss unhelpful behaviors, but it is the helpful behaviors that are discussed at length, recorded, and put on display for later reference.

Follow the same procedure for each new social skill that is introduced. Keep these sheets and post them each time group work is done. This saves time and serves as a constant visual reminder of appropriate group behavior. These sheets can be referred to and/or added to each time students work in groups.

OBSERVATION OF A SOCIAL SKILL

In this section, we examine the collection of observation data, as well as ways to organize and use this valuable information. (See Chapter 9 for how to share this information with students.)

The teacher observes students working in groups. S/he writes appropriate behaviors on a form. This provides students with data about social skill use.

Tell students before you start that you are recording their exact words and actions. Let them know that the observation form will be given privately to each group after work time is done. This announcement can reduce their possible fears of seeing you take notes. This more relaxed atmosphere can increase productivity.

The teacher moves from group to group writing notes each time the assigned social skill is observed. Not only do students benefit from actual data of appropriate behavior, but they also get the message that these behaviors are so important that the teacher will look and listen for them during work time. By observing their use of social skills during work time, the teacher demonstrates that in this classroom we do more than talk about social skills — we use them!

We recommend that you observe for social skills when:

* A new social skill is introduced.
* Student behavior in groups becomes disruptive and unproductive.
* You want to support continued use of a previously introduced social skill.

We have developed three observation forms to be used during group work time. Any of them can be used when a social skill has been assigned. Each sample form has been filled in to give you an idea of behaviors you might notice during work time. (See Appendix C for blank observation forms.)

ONE GROUP OBSERVATION FORM

Group Members' Names: _Jesse, Carlos, India_

Social Skill: _Check for Agreement_

Sounds Like	Looks Like
"What do you think?"	*Nod*
"I like this. Do you?"	*Point to paper*
"Okay?"	*Shake head*
Chuckle	*Smile*

One Group Observation Form

As you move from group to group, write down the exact words you hear and the specific behaviors you see that fit the assigned social skill. Remain long enough or return later in order to record something for every group. This helps even the most reluctant group feel that they are experiencing some success.

Multi-Group Observation Form

The second form is used when you have many groups to observe and not much time to spend with each group. Use in the same way as the previous form. When you use this observation form, you can record behaviors for several groups at a time. *After* group work time you cut the form apart and give each group only their separate strip. (See Chapter 9 for use of this data.)

MULTI-GROUP OBSERVATION FORM
Social Skill: *Disagree in an Agreeable Way*

Group Names	Sounds Like	Looks Like
Eric *Lacey* *Ieshia*	*"I guess so."* *"Let's add..."* *"I'd like this one better."*	*Nod* *Smile*
Tiffany *Tyler* *Lupita* *Sara*	*"No, I don't think so."* *"Okay, for this time."* *"Yup, I'll change my mind."*	*Write idea* *Point to paper* *Smile*
Trey *Carina* *Katelyn*	*"That's fine."* *"I'll go for it if you will."* *"I'm not sure."*	*Shake head* *Relaxed face*

Classroom Observation Form

This next form does not have any student names on it. You use one form on paper or on a transparency and record positive behaviors wherever you hear and see them. For this observation it is not necessary to record who used each skill.

CLASSROOM OBSERVATION FORM	
Social Skill: *Keep Track of Time*	
Sounds Like	**Looks Like**
"Let's keep going."	*Point to the clock*
"Can we move on to #3?"	*Move paper and pencil to next writer in the group*
"We're right on time."	

When you begin to use the observation forms, you may notice students being phony with one another as they use the social skill. Felicia might say, "That was a GREAT idea," in a sing-song voice. Trey might say, "I like that," and then ask you, "Did you write that down?" We suggest that you do write the exaggerated or fake practice in the beginning. After all, isn't that better than the "real" impolite words? After awhile, announce that you are only going to record the authentic behaviors. As the students practice these skills, the behaviors will become more natural.

ORGANIZATION AND USE OF OBSERVATION DATA

You and the students go to a lot of trouble to examine observation data. It would be a shame to just throw it away. We have two suggestions for keeping track of that valuable information.

Class List. You have already started a "Sounds Like/Looks Like" list for social skills. Record any helpful behaviors you noticed during your observations which are not already listed on chart paper. You may have heard some new ways to check for understanding, for example, or seen some different ways students have encouraged one another. Record these while students are processing or as you mention them during your feedback. Also record additional behaviors students notice. If these specific words and actions are reviewed before the next cooperative lesson, they serve as a reminder of appropriate behavior.

Group Folders. If groups are staying together for several activities, a group folder helps keep all written information organized. The folder may contain goals for social skills, unfinished work, corrected work, as well as observation forms. These observation forms are useful as evidence of growth in social skills as well as an indication of areas needing improvement.

SOCIAL SKILLS: THE GOAL

Task skills. Maintenance skills. Will you always have to teach, assign, and observe social skills when using cooperative groups? The answer is "No!" These three procedures are techniques to insure that students understand and practice the skills of cooperation. The ultimate goal is that students will cooperate, whether or not they are assigned skills or are working in a cooperative group that was structured and organized by a teacher.

Eventually you will not have to attend to social skills. But how will you know when it is time to phase them out? These are some behaviors that you might notice:

- You see nods, smiles, students leaning into the work.
- You hear kind words like, "We're off task, let's get back to work," and a groupmate answers, "Thanks, Tom, for reminding us."
- You notice the isolated student joining in the group work and liking it; the "boss" asking for someone else's opinion; papers being handed in on time because everyone helped.

When you reach this point, you will want to use social skill practice when a situation calls for it, such as problems with individuals, groups, or the class.

Having reached the ultimate goal, you will be ready to say, "Here is your cooperative group assignment. GO!" And they will.

TEACHING THE PROCESSING
OF SOCIAL SKILLS

Assigning social skills for students to practice will result in the improvement of your classroom groups. You will notice students talking to one another more, using more encouraging words, and sharing materials more often. If, however, you want to obtain maximum results for your efforts, we recommend that you include the strategy of processing after every cooperative group lesson.

Processing is a procedure by which students examine how they practiced a social skill, how they could use it more effectively next time, as well as where else in their lives this skill might be helpful. Processing on a consistent basis increases the use of positive group behaviors and also decreases the number of times social skills must be practiced before they become integrated into your students' behavior patterns.

Without processing, cooperative groups are often only groups of students sitting together working on the same task, rather than groups of students learning how to cooperate. Most classroom teachers trained in cooperative learning realize that there is only limited improvement on social skills without processing.

A ninth grade drafting teacher told us that he could not understand why his students continued to use many unfriendly behaviors during group work. He was especially puzzled because he had built in social skills and positive interdependence, but he had not seen the consistent improvement in student behaviors he had expected. The problem was revealed by his response to our question, "How do they deal with these unhelpful behaviors and the negative feelings they produce during processing?" His answer was, "Oh, we rarely have time for processing." After a brief review he realized that what seemed like a negative group experience could have been a source of learning. This teacher began to schedule time for processing in order to give his students the opportunity to learn from their group experiences.

CHAPTER 9

In this chapter we discuss how to set up processing experiences so that students analyze and evaluate their social skill behavior. From these learnings they can set goals or apply new understandings to other group situations. Your role is to encourage students to express their own opinions about their behavior and to process the group experiences they have lived. Later in the chapter we describe how you can share your observations and opinions in ways that allow your students to trust their own perceptions while helping them improve their skills. Processing time then becomes an opportunity for you to help your students grow toward independent thinking and problem-solving.

In this chapter we also discuss specific steps and methods to help you and your students have a successful experience with processing. Although careful pre-planning may prevent common problems from occurring, sometimes preventive measures are not effective. For that reason, in the last section of this chapter, we describe problems that may occur during processing. A range of possibilities for you to consider in finding your own solutions is also provided.

USE OF PROCESSING STATEMENTS

There are many methods for conducting processing with students of all ages. Our most successful method is when students respond to statements.

Processing begins as soon as the subject matter has been completed or work time is over. Even if the work will be continued in the next session, each day's use of a social skill is processed immediately. Allow 4-6 minutes before the end of the allotted cooperative group time for processing. Some teachers write the time on the board or set a timer so that everyone knows when it is time to stop and process. You will also need time to check papers, hand in work, and/or clean up. The teacher gives students one statement regarding use of the assigned social skill. Students respond by either filling in the blanks or making a choice as directed by the statement.

Students respond with a word or phrase to fill in the blank or finish the sentence.

Example: "We did well on '_____' by
                                                               (social skill)
_____, _____, and
_____."
                                    (3 specific behaviors)

Choosing a Processing Statement

The selection of a statement for use during processing depends upon several factors, including the reading skill level of students, time available and the teacher's desire for a varied approach. Less skilled readers may respond non-verbally or orally. Skilled readers are more able to offer written responses. Even though your students are capable of responding in writing, do not hesitate to have them use Values Voting, for example, when time is limited or a change of pace is in order. (See alternatives later in this chapter.)

Selecting by Focus. You will choose the point of focus when students are processing. Do they focus on self, others, or the group as a whole? In the first few cooperative group lessons, we suggest that you have students focus on the group as a whole. Use statements that deal with "we," "us," and "our group." This focus is recommended since it is easier to analyze "us" than "me" or "you." (See Chapters 5 & 6 for details about beginning processing statements and procedure.) After students have experienced cooperative groups and processing sessions several times, ask them to focus on themselves ("what I did") or on each other ("what you did") as well as on the group as a whole.

Processing Statements. When you select a specific statement to which students respond, you focus the processing procedure. If you ask, "How did you do in your groups today?" students will answer, "Fine," "Good," or "Great." That general, wishy-washy processing is worthless! Skip it and be specific instead.

- We did well on _____ by _____, (social skill)   (3 specific behaviors)
  _____, and _____ .

- I really felt good when others in my group _____ .

- I liked the way I helped my group today by _____ .

- In any group it is helpful to _____ because (social skill)
  _____ .

- Words we used to _____ were _____, (social skill)   (3 specific behaviors)
  _____, and _____ .

- Next time we can do more _____ by _____, (social skill)   (3 specific behaviors)
  _____, and _____ .

- You helped our group _____ by _____ and (social skill)   (2 specific behaviors)
  _____ .

These statements (and others in Appendix D) direct students to use thinking skills of analysis, application, or goal setting.

Analysis means that all responses deal with the group experience just completed. It is an attempt to help students discover what was a help and what was a hindrance in completing the day's group work. Students analyze whether specific behaviors had a positive or negative effect on group progress or morale.

Application deals with what students learned from this group experience that could be applied to other situations. Often teachers erroneously assume that students understand the connections between what happens in the classroom and what happens in the rest of their world. Using social skills in cooperative groups does not guarantee their use in other classroom activities, in the hallway, on the playground, or in the cafeteria. By including processing in cooperative groups, we provide opportunities for students to make connections between classroom cooperation and cooperative experiences in the rest of their lives. It helps them examine group interactions at school, home, place of worship, and in the community. Only by understanding the value of cooperation will students apply these lessons to other places besides the second-hour math class or the Tuesday reading lesson.

Goal setting gives students an opportunity to choose a specific social skill to use more effectively during the next cooperative group lesson. This is either a skill that they have not mastered or one they have practiced before but did not use in today's lesson. We recommend that you choose **one** processing statement to fit students' immediate social skill needs and to provide variety of discussion and thinking.

PROCEDURE FOR USING
PROCESSING STATEMENTS

1. The teacher picks one statement to focus students' thoughts and discussion. Show as well as tell your students the statement by putting it on the board or a transparency.

2. Each student responds to statement in small group so that everyone is heard from.

3. Responses are discussed within each group. Each person is ready to report the consensus decision.

4. Each group gives a report to the whole class. The reporter is picked at random or by the teacher. New positive behaviors are added to the social skill chart paper by the teacher.

5. Teacher feedback comes next. Observation form information is read to groups or given to them. Comments from the teacher are given as the last step.

ALTERNATIVES TO USING PROCESSING STATEMENTS

Use of processing statements is not the only way to help students reflect on their use of social skills. Use the alternative methods below when you want variety or time is short.

Alternative Procedure. Alternative methods require an alternative procedure.

1. The teacher picks one sentence to focus processing.

2. Students respond by Forced Choice, Values Voting, or Continuums within their own group.

3. Groups give a report to the whole class (all groups or some chosen by random method). Patterns in responses are discussed briefly (guided by teacher).

4. Teacher feedback comes last: first from observation forms and then from teacher comments.

Sample Sentences:

"Others in the group helped me when I had a question."

"We disagreed in a respectful way."

"I used names when talking to my groupmates."

"I felt encouraged in my group today."

"Today as a group, we accomplished our goal."

Forced Choice. Students make a choice between a set of two or three responses. The teacher reads each sentence (see samples above) from the board or a duplicated copy. Students respond by marking one choice, responding orally, or choosing non-verbally. We observed a group of kindergarten students draw a happy face on one side of a paper plate and a sad face on the opposite side. They then used these "signs" to indicate their responses to the sentences.

Sample sets of responses:

Never / Sometimes / Always

No / Yes

A Little / Some / A Lot
O   O   O   (fill in the circle)

Values Voting. The teacher tells students the response choices for voting. (Writing or drawing them on the board is helpful.) Each sentence (see samples above) is read aloud. Think time is given. Then everyone votes at the same time when the teacher says "Vote." This procedure helps prevent students voting the way their friends do and encourages them to express their own opinions.

Choices for Responses from Simple to More Complex:

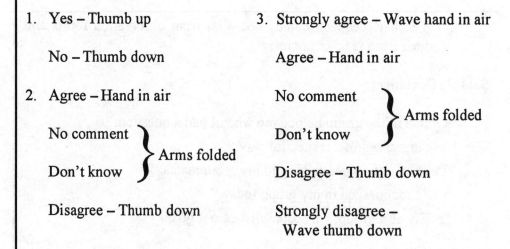

1. Yes – Thumb up

    No – Thumb down

2. Agree – Hand in air

    No comment }
    Don't know } Arms folded

    Disagree – Thumb down

3. Strongly agree – Wave hand in air

    Agree – Hand in air

    No comment }
    Don't know } Arms folded

    Disagree – Thumb down

    Strongly disagree –
      Wave thumb down

Continuums. Students put an "X" somewhere on the line between "Always" and "Never." This indicates how successful they feel they were on the social skill assigned for that day's lesson.

ALWAYS   NEVER

Continuums can be done on paper or by making a human continuum along a wall or line on the classroom floor. Both ends of the line are identified and students place themselves on the line where they feel their "X" belongs.

GIVING FEEDBACK

At this point, you have collected data on one of the observation forms: One Group; Multi-Group; or Classroom (Chapter 8). After you have observed and your students have done their processing, it is time for you to share the information collected. We recommend the following 7-step procedure for giving this feedback to students.

Step 1. Give the observation form to each group (read aloud to non-readers), or show your transparency form to the whole class.

Step 2. Allow 1-2 minutes for students in groups to see, hear, and discuss your data.

Step 3. Ask group reporters to tell new behaviors that can be added to the chart paper.

Step 4. Briefly tell your conclusions and perceptions of helpful and unhelpful behaviors that you noticed.

Step 5. Processing sheets and/or written observation forms are filed in folder for each group. Before the next session of cooperative group work, students can refer to these processing sheets and observation forms or the teacher can review the behaviors recorded on chart paper. This helps students focus on appropriate social skill behavior before they begin group work.

Step 6. Process the subject matter.

Step 7. The teacher does his/her own processing after the completed cooperative learning lesson.

Students' Opinions During Processing

In order for students to feel safe in risking their opinions, an atmosphere of trust and acceptance must be established. You can create this atmosphere in your classroom by discussing and enforcing the following guidelines whenever students are invited to publicly respond. These guidelines for teachers and students apply whether the reaction is an oral response, a vote, or choosing a spot on the continuum.

- All answers are acceptable.
- All positions are respected, whether agreed with or not.
- No group members may force anyone else to agree with their answer.
- There are no negative comments about one's self or others.

It is as important to follow these guidelines yourself as it is to make sure your students follow them. It is important for you to withhold your judgment of student responses, whether you agree or disagree. Students will be watching you closely. If you say, "Good!" to some responses, and say nothing about or frown at others, students will quickly learn that all answers are *not* acceptable.

For example, if a group of students votes that they stayed on task and you know that they barely started on the assigned work, accept their opinion with no comment. Later, in private, you could share your observations and opinions. At that time you may have them confront the discrepancy. Give students the space to risk their own points of view even though it may sometimes be uncomfortable for you.

Teacher Opinions After Student Processing

As we have described how to set up processing sessions so that your students can learn from their experiences, we have asked you to hold onto your opinions until your students have had an opportunity to express theirs. Now it is your turn! The challenge is to present your opinions and feedback so that your students feel respected, encouraged, and motivated to apply their learnings.

Students are so used to hearing teacher opinions, judgments, praise, criticism, suggestions, directions, and advice, that it is easy for them to develop the habit of not thinking for themselves. They may find that not only is it easier to wait for the teacher's opinion, but usually the teacher's opinion is the only one that counts! Rarely do students have the opportunity to give their opinions about their own work; even more rarely are those opinions solicited by the teacher. Small wonder that when students are asked for their opinions about their behaviors during processing, they are usually either reluctant or unskilled at giving them. This is why we recommend that you give your feedback after students give theirs. If you go first with your observations, students may copy what you have noticed and attempt to produce the "right" answer. If you go first with your opinions about helpful and unhelpful behaviors, students have no need to analyze themselves and the success of their groups.

If you want to help students think for themselves, processing time is an important opportunity. We hear teachers everywhere ask, "Why won't my students think for themselves? They're always asking me if something is long enough, short enough, red enough, blue enough, neat enough. Enough! Why can't they trust their own opinions?" The reason is that we teachers have taught them to turn to us for evaluation of their work. As a result, they have not learned to form their own opinions and trust their own perceptions.

One of the ways you can help students learn how to be more confident of themselves and their opinions is by changing the ways you react to their responses. The ways that teachers praise and criticize have a profound effect on student's self-images, confidence, and achievement.* Be conscious of your words and behaviors, and use some different ways to share your opinions. You can more effectively motivate students to reach their potential and trust themselves by using such methods.

We have found that in order for teacher input to be the most beneficial to students' growth, it needs to be:

- Planned
- Specific
- Consistent
- Brief
- Timely

---

*Arthur L. Costa. *The School As A Home For The Mind.* Palatine, IL: Skylight Publishing. 1991.

If teacher input is haphazard and non-specific, students often do not pay attention. They are likely to "tune out" the teacher's voice. To encourage students to "tune in," consider the following methods of giving your feedback and opinions on student behavior. Then decide how you can best give students information which they can use to congratulate themselves for the work just completed as well as to improve future efforts.

Praise. What is so difficult about telling students about the behaviors they exhibited which helped the group? Praise comes easily to teachers. What concerns us is that the type of praise you give can create very different outcomes. One type of praise is called evaluative and the other is called descriptive.*

Evaluative praise sounds like:
"Your groups did a really good job today."

Descriptive praise sounds like:
"I heard people saying 'Please' and 'Thank you' in your group today. I saw materials being shared by everyone. These behaviors helped your groups work well together."

Evaluative praise shows teacher approval but gives no specifics in terms of appropriate behavior. Descriptive praise describes these behaviors as well as their effect. Using evaluative praise creates a short-term benefit because students are often motivated by it. Words like "excellent," "great," "fantastic," "wonderful," all give students immediate teacher approval. The problem is that long-term evaluative praise creates dependency on the teacher. Students must continually check with you to make sure that they receive your approval.

Descriptive praise can be equally as motivational once students get used to it. It requires some practice for students to acquire the knack of hearing your descriptive words and then saying to themselves, "I did a good job," or "We really were great at cooperating today." This sort of self-praise results in a long- term benefit because students become their own sources of approval. They no longer feel compelled to look to the teacher for measures of their success.

---

*Adele Faber & Elaine Mazlish. *How To Talk So Kids Will Listen & Listen So Kids Will Talk.* New York, NY: Rawson, Wade Publishers. 1980.

Evaluative praise can also create feelings of competition and hostility within a classroom because of labeling, judging, and comparing.

"Group 2 is the best today because they finished first. Great job!"

"Sarah did more encouraging than anyone else today. She's terrific!"

Those who do not receive praise may work harder to earn it the next time. However, in such cases, students are still dependent on the teacher's approval. This does not help them trust their own opinions. Even labeling the entire class as "good" is not as effective as telling them specifically about observed behaviors which were friendly, polite, or helpful. When you give descriptive praise to students in the privacy of their small groups, look at the individual, use his or her name, and tell how this individual's behavior in the group contributed to the outcomes for the group.

"Jim, your encouraging Sean seemed to help him keep working. When you said, 'You can do it!' he smiled, sat straight, took a breath, and continued with his spelling work."

If you praise the class, do it descriptively rather than evaluatively.

"I noticed that your groups worked effectively today. People expressed their ideas and when someone didn't, he or she was asked for his or her opinion. That helped everyone stay involved."

The examples below further illustrate the difference between evaluative and descriptive praise. Notice which type of praise would be more useful to students in recognizing the positive behaviors which you would like to see continued.

Evaluative Praise	**Descriptive Praise**
"Good work on social skills."	*"I saw smiles and eye contact. Everyone cheered when the work was finished. Your group acted like a team."*
"Excellent work in your groups today."	*"You shared materials in your group. People took turns. I heard soft voices. Your group helped our classroom stay relaxed and calm."*

Evaluative Praise	**Descriptive Praise**
"I'm proud of your groups."	*"Group members disagreed with one another in friendly ways. People paraphrased, nodded, and smiled to show group members they were heard. I understand why your groups get along so well."*

Criticism. During this step of processing, you can also describe to students the unhelpful behaviors you noticed during work time. Just as it is important to praise descriptively, it is important to criticize descriptively.

Descriptive criticism gives students information about behaviors that are disruptive to the group.

"When you wouldn't take your turn to read, Madeline, you did not contribute to the group. That was not helpful behavior."

Evaluative criticism labels students and can create resentment and resistance. "You were uncooperative, Madeline. I'm shocked at your behavior."

Criticism that encourages students to change their behavior has the following characteristics:

- ◆ Focuses on the behavior rather than on the person. "You're rude," focuses on Joaquin as a person. "You interrupted Marisa three times when she started to give her opinion," focuses on Joaquin's behavior.

- ◆ Involves sharing information rather than giving advice or threatening. "I don't like people being called 'Stupid' or 'Dummy.' I expect you to settle your differences by discussion, not name-calling." This descriptive criticism leaves students the space to decide what to do with the information and how to improve. "You'd better knock off the name-calling or you'll stay after school," allows little room for students to decide what to do or how to do it.

- ◆ Involves only one or two behaviors. There may be many behaviors that you do not want students to continue. However, if you mention all of them, you reduce the possibility that students will be able to do *any* of them. Choose only one or two of the most crucial behaviors. Ignore the others for now.

♦ Is avoided when you or the other person have strong feelings such as anger, frustration, or impatience. It is more helpful to give criticism when everyone is calm. If emotions are running high, talk with the person or group later, or give your feedback the next day before group work begins.

Notice in the examples below the differences between descriptive and evaluative criticism.

Evaluative Criticism	**Descriptive Criticism**
"You did a poor job today."	*"I noticed people grabbing materials from one another. I saw frowns and heard angry words. That's not using social skills."*
"Don't ever let me catch you doing that again."	*"People who hit others will have to work alone."*
"You're a bunch of spoiled brats."	*"I saw people writing on each other's papers without permission. That's why some group members were angry."*

If you include criticism in your feedback to the class, mention behaviors only, not names. When you are sharing criticism privately in a small group, look at the person, say the person's name, and address the criticism to that individual. Resist labeling the group. ("You were all really mean to each other.")

If you feel that criticism is in order, do it descriptively and without mentioning names. ("People are not for hitting. Name calling and angry words do not settle arguments.") Sometimes individual conversations are needed after group work with only the person(s) involved in a negative situation.

Remember, the purpose of processing is to give students an opportunity to use their own intelligence and perception. It is not a time for the teacher to get on a bandwagon or a soapbox.

TEACHER PROCESSING OF THE LESSON

Just as students learn from processing their experiences, so do teachers, so take time to conduct your own processing. Immediately after class, or the same day, take five minutes to analyze the lesson. Determine what worked and what did not. Analyze your behavior and set goals for yourself. Could you use more teambuilding next time? Do you want the groups larger? Smaller? Would a 3-Step lesson work more effectively? What type of observation form would be most useful for you to use the next time? What method of processing would be appropriate? How can you interrupt groups less and let them work on their own more? How can you be more descriptive and less evaluative? By taking a few minutes to process your cooperative group experiences, you will have learned from what happened instead of wishing that group experiences had been "better."

Your processing of the lesson may also include decisions about which social skills to assign for the next cooperative group session. If students have done Goal Setting Processing, then they will already have one social skill on which to work. We recommend that you plan for your next cooperative learning lesson based on student processing results, observation data, and your own perceptions.

For example, when a group has difficulty being specific about which behaviors they used when practicing "Respond to Ideas," it could be that they did not practice that skill. The observation data you collected may indicate that you observed your students responding to ideas only once during the time you were there. Using your perceptions and observations, you may remember that one person filled out the answer sheet, only rarely consulting the other two groupmates. Based on all of this information, your conclusion could be to assign the social skill of "Share ideas and information" or "Check for agreement." These skills would encourage students to include everyone in the group process. As you continue to repeat this decision-making after each cooperative group lesson, notice, too, whether a group uses more maintenance or more task social skills. If group members continually have trouble getting along with one another, assign maintenance skills. If they often do not complete the work, put more emphasis on task skills. Use all of your resources as you continue to assess needs and assign social skills.

ROADBLOCKS TO PROCESSING

road block (rōd blăk) — *n., an element from outside or inside oneself that causes temporary difficulties in reaching a goal. syn. see obstacle, hurdle, challenge.*

Even though you have followed all of our suggestions and instructions for setting up and conducting processing, you may find that problems have surfaced (as they do every day in the classroom). As you can see from the above definition of roadblock (taken from the Dishon and Wilson O'Leary Unabridged Dictionary), we view these problems as only temporary setbacks. Even the best efforts to prevent roadblocks from occurring will not work 100% of the time. We encourage you to see sources of problems not as evidence of failure, but as challenges and a learning opportunities.

In this section we share the most common roadblocks that teachers run into when setting up and conducting processing sessions. Several possible remedies which have worked for other teachers are listed here. Look them over carefully to see if there are possibilities or suggestions that may be helpful for you. If not, use the list as a stepping stone toward finding your own answers.

Roadblock: Not Enough Time For Processing

There are numerous reasons for this problem. Fire drills, announcements, buses arriving late or departing early, unannounced assemblies, direction-giving that takes longer than planned — all of these situations influence your carefully planned and protected time for processing.

Possible Remedies:

- Do quick processing (Values Voting or Forced Choice).
- Finish work next time. Do processing now.
- Do processing next time.

Roadblock: Superficial Processing

This roadblock is evident when responses to processing are (1)vague or (2) when some students or groups are not involved in processing.

(1) **Answers Are Vague.** This occurs when you get the same answer repeated over and over; "Yes" or "No" answers with no explanation; or responses like "We cooperated," "We did OK," or "We did a good job."

Possible Remedies:

+ Use the processing statements suggested in this guidebook since they require students to be specific.
+ Create your own processing statements that require filling in blanks with specific words or phrases.
+ Allow enough time for processing so students can be more thoughtful.
+ Take time to press students into being more specific. "What does a 'good job' look like and sound like?"

(2) **Students Are Not Involved.** This happens when one person does the processing and all the others simply agree, or when someone does not offer any response.

Possible Remedies:

+ Do processing in writing.
+ Include processing as last answer on group answer sheet.
+ Each person does "I" Analysis Processing.
+ Student not involved in processing is assigned to be recorder/spokesperson for the group.
+ Students take turns being recorder.
+ All group members sign the Processing Sheet to show participation and agreement.

Roadblock: Students Do Not Use
Social Skills During Processing

This roadblock is in evidence when you hear arguing and negative comments, or when the group is not working as a team during processing.

Possible Remedies:

- Remind groups beforehand to use social skills.
- Teacher observes and makes notes. Reports on observations before next day's processing time.
- Assign a social skill during processing.

Roadblock: Students Hesitate to Give
Their Own Opinions

This roadblock occurs when students give you what they think you want to hear or when they wait for your opinion rather than risk sharing theirs.

Possible Remedies:

- Begin with Fill-in-the Blank processing; then move to more risky methods (Values Voting, Forced Choice, Continuums).
- Wait until students have processed before giving your opinions.
- Eliminate your evaluative praise or criticism.
- Give objective feedback with occasional descriptive praise or criticism.
- Persevere! Students need time and practice to trust you and to trust their own opinions.

SIGNS OF SUCCESS

Since processing takes much time and effort, it is important to be aware of the signs of success. You will know that processing is working when you notice *any* of the following:

- More students are involved in processing.
- Responses are clear and specific.
- Social skills are used during processing.
- Students give their opinions easily and candidly.
- You hear processing going on *before* and *after* processing time.
- Social skill behavior improves — in groups and elsewhere.

When you notice *most* of the behaviors above, you know that it is time to phase out formal processing of the social skills. Just as you phase out assigning specific social skills, the processing can become informal, too. You might occasionally ask a question of the whole group. ("What social skills were you conscious of using today?") or ask small groups to briefly discuss social skills ("What social skills would have been helpful to use in your group today?"). Trust that your skills, patience and effort will make processing a rewarding experience for you and your students. Even if students are reluctant, remember that you are training students in life-long skills. These skills will help your students learn from their experiences rather than repeat the same self-defeating behaviors day after day, year after year.

COOPERATIVE LEARNING: "TO BE CONTINUED"

This is the end of this guidebook. It is not the end of what you want or will need to know about cooperative learning. There are books and materials for you to examine as well as many areas for you to explore. A few of them are:

Support. Choose books, groups, associations to be involved with (see bibliography). Search out and join a cooperative learning support group. Decide what support you can ask for from teachers in your building or other experts who are available to you.

Role of the Administrator. Find out what your administrator knows about cooperative learning and what support s/he is able and willing to give you.

Parent Involvement. Parents can be your greatest support group when you inform them of your cooperative learning goals. Read our newsletter, *Cooperation Unlimited INK,* and other sources for on-going tips and techniques for parent involvement.

No matter how clumsy or skillful you feel with cooperative learning, imagine a time when cooperative learning is just a natural, flowing part of your classroom operation.

The way you use cooperative groups can change by the hour and the day. There may be a time in your room when:

- You work with a selected number of students while other students work in cooperative groups. On some days it might be necessary for you to have one-third or one-half of the class work with you in a directed-teaching situation. For example, a majority of the students need your attention to clarify the properties of the next five items on the Periodic Chart of Elements. That means that members of the class who have mastered that task or who only need to review may work in cooperative groups to complete a lab experiment involving an element from the chart.

- You facilitate one or two cooperative groups while the rest of the class works on individual assignments.

- You work individually with a large number of students on an assignment while one or two cooperative groups complete a separate project.

- You work with a small number of students on make-up work in one part of the room while other students work in cooperative groups.

The variations are many. Use our suggestions to construct your own foundation. Create routines to make the building of your cooperative classroom an enjoyable project and process!

Cooperative Learning
3-Step Lesson Plan Worksheet

Name _____ Class/Grade _____

Subject _____ # of Students _____

STEP 1. Subject Matter Content

    A.   Learning Objective:

          Information/Skill to be learned: _____

    B.   Group Goal: _____

    C.   Name of Strategy: _____

    D.   Learning Experience(s) that precedes group work (lesson, video, etc.)

          _____

    E.   Length of work time: _____ minutes

STEP 2. Group Composition and Room Arrangement

    A.   Group Size: _____

    B.   Assignment to Groups: (check one)

          ❏ Random - - - - - - - Method: _____

          ❏ Teacher-Selected - - - Criteria: _____ _____

    C.   Duration of Groups: _____

    D.   Room Arrangement: _____

STEP 3.   Positive Interdependence
(use as many as possible)

❑   A.   Materials   # Needed   Description

   ❑   Limited   _____   _____

   ❑   Jigsawed   _____   _____

❑   B.   One Product: _____

❑   C.   Common Goal: _____

❑   D.   Rotate Roles: _____   _____   _____

Step 4.   Individual Accountability

❑   A.   Signatures (on front)

❑   B.   Random Check (explain method)_____

❑   C.   Individual performance (explain) _____

From *A Guidebook for Cooperative Learning* by Dee Dishon and Pat Wilson O'Leary. Holmes Beach, FL: Learning Publications, Inc., 1994.

Step 5.   **Subject Matter Directions:** (State in language your students will understand.)

"Your group will work cooperatively to:

1. _____

2. _____

3. _____

4. _____

5. _____

6. _____ "

_____ minutes work time

Where to display for students: ❑ easel   ❑ chalkboard   ❑ screen

Step 6.   **Process Subject Matter**
          (after work time)

❑   Hear responses (all or some)

❑   See products (all or some)

❑   Students check products

❑   Hand in products

❑   Discussion of academic skills

Cooperative Learning
5-Step Lesson Plan Worksheet

Name _____ Class/Grade _____

Subject _____ # of Students _____

STEP 1. **Subject Matter Content**

    A.   Learning Objective:

            Information/Skill to be learned: _____

    B.   Group Goal: _____

    C.   Name of Strategy (if applicable): _____

    D.   Learning Experience(s) that precedes group work (lesson, video, etc.)

            _____

    E.   Length of work time: _____ minutes

STEP 2. **Group Composition and Room Arrangement**

    A.   Group Size: _____

    B.   Assignment to Groups: (check one)

        ❑   Random – – – – – – Method: _____

        ❑   Teacher-Selected – – – Criteria: _____ _____

    C.   Duration of Groups: _____

    D.   Room Arrangement: _____

STEP 3.   Positive Interdependence

❑   A.   Materials   # Needed   Description

      ❑   Limited   _____   _____

      ❑   Jigsawed   _____   _____

❑   B.   One Product: _____

❑   C.   Common Goal: _____

❑   D.   Rotate Roles: _____   _____   _____

❑   E.   Reward: _____   Criteria for receiving: _____

      Reason to use: _____

Step 4.   Individual Accountability

A.   Signatures (on front)

B.   Random Check (explain method) _____

C.   Individual performance (explain) _____

Step 5.   Subject Matter Directions: (State in language your students will understand.)

"Your group will work cooperatively to:

1. _____

2. _____

3. _____

4. _____

From *A Guidebook for Cooperative Learning* by Dee Dishon and Pat Wilson O'Leary. Holmes Beach, FL: Learning Publications, Inc., 1994.

5. _____

6. _____ ''

_____ minutes work time

Where to display for students: ❑ easel   ❑ chalkboard   ❑ screen

Step 6.   Social Skill

_____   Teacher-Used Observation Form:

❑ One Group
❑ Multi-Group
❑ Classroom

Step 7.   Process Social Skill (after work time)
(Choose one statement for students to complete)

❑ We did well on _____ by _____, _____, and _____.
              (social skill)   (specific behaviors)

❑ I liked the way I helped my group today by _____.

❑ In any group it is helpful to _____ because _____.
                         (social skill)

Step 8.   Process Subject Matter (after work time)

❑ Hear responses (all or some)

❑ See products (all or some)

❑ Students check products

❑ Hand in products

❑ Discussion of academic skills

From *A Guidebook for Cooperative Learning* by Dee Dishon and Pat Wilson O'Leary. Holmes Beach, FL: Learning Publications, Inc., 1994.

One Group Observation Form

Group Members' Names: _____

Social Skill: _____

SOUNDS LIKE	LOOKS LIKE

From *A Guidebook for Cooperative Learning* by Dee Dishon and Pat Wilson O'Leary. Holmes Beach, FL: Learning Publications, Inc., 1994.

Multi-Group Observation Form

Social Skill: _____

GROUP NAMES	SOUNDS LIKE	LOOKS LIKE
_____ _____ _____ _____		
_____ _____ _____ _____		
_____ _____ _____ _____		
_____ _____ _____ _____		
_____ _____ _____ _____		
_____ _____ _____ _____		

From *A Guidebook for Cooperative Learning* by Dee Dishon and Pat Wilson O'Leary. Holmes Beach, FL: Learning Publications, Inc., 1994.

Classroom Observation Form

Social Skill: _____

SOUNDS LIKE	LOOKS LIKE

From *A Guidebook for Cooperative Learning* by Dee Dishon and Pat Wilson O'Leary. Holmes Beach, FL: Learning Publications, Inc., 1994.

Choices for Processing Social Skills
(See Chapter 9 for directions on how to use)

Examples of Processing Statements

Analysis Processing:

About Self:

Fill in the Blank/Finish the Sentence

1. Ways I used the social skill most consistently today are _____

   by _____, _____, and _____.
   <small>(three specific behaviors)</small>

2. I enjoyed practicing today's social skill of _____ because

   _____.

3. When someone in my group was not contributing, I _____

   _____.

About Others:

Fill in the Blank/Finish the Sentence

1. Someone who took turns was _____.
   <small>(name)</small>

2. The most helpful thing someone did in our group on the social skill of _____

   was _____.

3. I really felt good when others in my group _____

   _____.

4. _____, I enjoyed it when you _____
   <small>(name)</small>

   _____.

From *A Guidebook for Cooperative Learning* by Dee Dishon and Pat Wilson O'Leary. Holmes Beach, FL: Learning Publications, Inc., 1994.

About Us:

Fill in the Blank/Finish the Sentence

1. Our group did well on _____ by _____,
    (social skill)   (three specific behaviors)
    _____, and _____.

2. The words we used to _____ were _____.
    (social skill)
    _____.
    _____.
    (specific words)

3. We enjoyed practicing today's social skill of _____ because
    _____.

4. We could do better on _____ by _____.
    (social skill)

5. Today we really needed someone in our group to _____.
    (social behavior)

6. We checked for agreement (reached consensus, etc.) by _____,
    (three specific behaviors)
    _____, and _____.

Application Processing:

About Individual or Group:

1. One thing I/we learned or relearned about group work is _____
    _____.

2. I/we learned the following ways to _____:
    (social skill)
    _____, _____, and _____.
    (three specific behaviors)

3. I/we learned that in any group it is helpful to _____.

From *A Guidebook for Cooperative Learning* by Dee Dishon and Pat Wilson O'Leary. Holmes Beach, FL: Learning Publications, Inc., 1994.

(The following can be responded to individually or by the group as a whole.)

4.   The social skill we used that can be transferred to any group is _____

_____.

5.   The social skill of _____ could be used at other times like

_____.

6.   Sometimes it's better for two or three people to solve a problem rather than one because

_____.

7.   It is important to _____ in other places besides the classroom because
                            (social skill)

_____.

Goal Setting Processing (use when two or more social skills have been introduced to the group).

1.   One social skill I/we will practice more consistently next time is _____

_____.

     I/we will do this by _____, _____, and
                                    (three specific behaviors)

_____.

2.   The social skill I/we want to be sure to use next time is _____ because

_____.

3.   Our group will _____ next time we meet in a group by
                          (social skill)

_____.
                          (specific behavior)

From *A Guidebook for Cooperative Learning* by Dee Dishon and Pat Wilson O'Leary. Holmes Beach, FL: Learning Publications, Inc., 1994.

FORCED CHOICE, VALUES VOTING, OR CONTINUUMS

Sentences to use for specific social skill assigned.

About Self:

I encouraged others.

I followed directions.

I responded to others' ideas.

I helped others in my group to understand the work.

I used names.

I asked questions when I didn't understand something.

About Others:

My ideas were responded to even if they were not agreed with or used.

Others looked at me when I was talking.

I felt encouraged in my group today.

Others in the group helped me when I had a question.

Others shared their materials with me.

About Us:

Today as a group we:

+ accomplished our goal
+ helped each other
+ felt good about working together
+ kept each other and ourselves on task
+ disagreed in a nice way
+ accepted each others' ideas
+ took turns

From *A Guidebook for Cooperative Learning* by Dee Dishon and Pat Wilson O'Leary. Holmes Beach, FL: Learning Publications, Inc., 1994.

SAMPLE PROCESSING SHEETS

1.   Forced Choice

    A.   Others shared with me

        ☺   ☹

    B.   I encouraged others in my group.

        ☺   ☹

2.   Values Voting

		A little	Some	A lot
A.	We helped each other	○	○	○
B.	We shared ideas	○	○	○

3.   Continuums

We _____ equally.
                (social skill)

     ☺   😐   ☹

   Always   Some   Never

From *A Guidebook for Cooperative Learning* by Dee Dishon and Pat Wilson O'Leary. Holmes Beach, FL: Learning Publications, Inc., 1994.

Primary

Friendship Skills	A little	Some	A lot
1. We helped each other.	O	O	O
2. We shared ideas.	O	O	O
3. We smiled at each other.	O	O	O
4. We worked together until the task was done.	O	O	O

Upper Elementary/Junior High

Put an X on the line where you think you or your group performed on the social skill in today's lesson.

1. I responded to others' ideas.

_____

ALWAYS   NEVER

2. Others responded to my ideas.

_____

ALWAYS   NEVER

3. Three ways we responded to ideas.

_____, _____, and _____.

Senior High/Adult

Fill in the blanks with a word or phrase that your group best feels completes the sentences.

We used the social skill of _____ by

_____, _____, and _____.

The social skill we want to be sure to use next time is _____

because _____

_____.

From *A Guidebook for Cooperative Learning* by Dee Dishon and Pat Wilson O'Leary. Holmes Beach, FL: Learning Publications, Inc., 1994.

Lesson Plan Samples

Four sample lesson plans are included as guides to help you be creative about the lessons you can teach using cooperative groups. As you look over each of these plans, consider the basic skills or concepts which you teach that could be implemented using the particular lesson plan. Consider how each could be adapted to your grade level and/or subject area. Keep in mind the specific materials that you have available and the objectives you plan to cover this semester/school year.

Check back with Chapter 4 (positive interdependence and individual accountability), and Chapters 5 and 6 (planning and implementing a 5-step lesson) as you put theory into practice. (If you are interested in using these plans for 3-step lessons, simply omit Steps 6 and 7 from our samples.)

Cooperative Learning
5-Step Lesson Plan Worksheet

Name _____ Class/Grade *K-1*

Subject *Matching* _____ # of Students _____

STEP 1. Subject Matter Content

    A.   Learning Objective:

        Information/Skill to be learned: *Matching geometric shapes*

    B.   Group Goal: *Create poster with pictures of similar shape*

    C.   Name of Strategy (if applicable): _____

    D.   Learning Experience(s) that precedes group work (lesson, video, etc.)

        Review of shapes and practice with matching

    E.   Length of work time: *10* minutes

STEP 2. Group Composition and Room Arrangement

    A.   Group Size: *3*

    B.   Assignment to Groups (choose one):

    ❑   Random – – – – – – – Method: _____

    ☒   Teacher-Selected – – – Criteria: *boys/girls; different skill levels*

    C.   Duration of Groups: *3 weeks*

    D.   Room Arrangement: *Seated in circle on floor, space between groups*

STEP 3.   Positive Interdependence

☒ A.   Materials   # Needed   Description

      ☒   Limited   _____1_____   _scissors & glue stick_____
                                           _construction paper_____
                                           _3-5 magazines_____

      ❑   Jigsawed   _____   _____

☒ B.   One Product: _poster with examples of assigned shape_

☒ C.   Common Goal: _each student contributes and agrees with shapes chosen_

☒ D.   Rotate Roles: _cutter_____   __paster_____   _____

❑ E.   Reward: _____   Criteria for receiving: _____

      Reason to use: _____

STEP 4.   Individual Accountability

☒ A.   Signatures (on front)

❑ B.   Random Check (explain method) _____

❑ C.   Individual performance (explain) _____

STEP 5.   Subject Matter Directions: State in language your students will understand.

Your group will work cooperatively to:

1. _Find several items in magazines that have same shape your group is assigned._____

2. _Check with each groupmate to be sure everyone agrees that shape is correct._____

3. _Cutter cuts out picture._____

From *A Guidebook for Cooperative Learning* by Dee Dishon and Pat Wilson O'Leary. Holmes Beach, FL: Learning Publications, Inc., 1994.

4.   *Paster pastes it on paper after everyone agrees.*

5.   *Everyone gets a turn to find shape, cut and paste.*

6.   *Keep going until time is up. Then you will all sign to show agreement.*

    10   minutes work time

Where to display for students: ❑ easel   ❑ chalkboard   ☒ screen

STEP 6.   Social Skill

Check for Agreement

Teacher-Used Observation Form:

❑ One Group
❑ Multi-Group
☒ Classroom

STEP 7.   Process Social Skill (after work time)
(Choose one statement for students to complete)

❑ We did well on _____ by _____, _____, and _____ .
                (social skill)   (specific behaviors)

☒ I liked the way I helped my group today by _____ .

❑ In any group it is helpful to _____ because _____ .
                         (social skill)

STEP 8.   Process Subject Matter (after work time)

❑ Hear responses (all or some)

☒   See products (all or *some*)

❑ Students check products

☒   Hand in products

❑ Discussion of academic skills

From *A Guidebook for Cooperative Learning* by Dee Dishon and Pat Wilson O'Leary. Holmes Beach, FL: Learning Publications, Inc., 1994.

Cooperative Learning
5-Step Lesson Plan Worksheet

Name _____ Class/Grade ___*2-3*___

Subject __*Math*_____ # of Students _____

STEP 1.   Subject Matter Content

   A.   Learning Objective:

         Information/Skill to be learned: ___*Balancing objects; reaching conclusions*___

   B.   Group Goal: ___*Balance several objects and draw conclusions about balancing*___

   C.   Name of Strategy (if applicable): _____

   D.   Learning Experience(s) that precedes group work (lesson, video, etc.)

         ___*Showing how balancing equipment works*_____

   E.   Length of work time: ___*12*___ minutes

STEP 2.   Group Composition and Room Arrangement

   A.   Group Size: ___*3*___

   B.   Assignment to Groups (choose one):

         ☒   Random – – – – – – – Method: ___*Names from "Winner's Basket"*___

         ❑   Teacher-Selected – – – Criteria: _____

   C.   Duration of Groups: ___*6 weeks*_____

   D.   Room Arrangement: ___*Chairs around one group desk; space between groups*___

From *A Guidebook for Cooperative Learning* by Dee Dishon and Pat Wilson O'Leary. Holmes Beach, FL: Learning Publications, Inc., 1994.

STEP 3.   Positive Interdependence

    ☒   A.   Materials   # Needed   Description

            ☒   Limited   *1*   *balance beam; pencil*
                                     1   *piece of paper*
                                 several   *blocks; objects*

            ❑   Jigsawed

    ☒   B.   One Product: *written conclusions*

    ☒   C.   Common Goal: *each student works and agrees with balance conclusions*

    ☒   D.   Rotate Roles: *writer*

    ❑   E.   Reward: _____   Criteria for receiving: _____

                Reason to use: _____

STEP 4.   Individual Accountability

    ☒   A.   Signatures (on front)

    ☒   B.   Random Check (explain method):   *"Winner's Basket" for group reporter*

    ❑   C.   Individual performance (explain) _____

STEP 5.   Subject Matter Directions: State in language your students will understand.

Your group will work cooperatively to:

1.   *Balance as many items as you can.*

2.   *Check with each groupmate to be sure everyone agrees that items balance.*

3.   *Each take turn writing conclusions on paper after everyone agrees.*

From *A Guidebook for Cooperative Learning* by Dee Dishon and Pat Wilson O'Leary. Holmes Beach, FL: Learning Publications, Inc., 1994.

4.   *Everyone gets a turn to balance and write.*

5.   *Keep going until time is up.*

6.   *Everyone will sign to show agreement.*

    12   minutes work time

Where to display for students: ❏ easel   ❏ chalkboard   ☒ screen

STEP 6.   Social Skill

                                                Teacher-Used Observation Form:

   Answer back politely   ☒   One Group
                                        ❏   Multi-Group
                                        ❏   Classroom

STEP 7.   Process Social Skill (after work time)
            (Choose one statement for students to complete)

☒   We did well on   *answering back politely*   by _____, _____, and _____.
                      (social skill)   (specific behaviors)

❏   I liked the way I helped my group today by _____.

❏   In any group it is helpful to _____ because _____.
                                 (social skill)

STEP 8.   Process Subject Matter (after work time)

❏   Hear responses (all or some)

☒   See products (all or *some*)

❏   Students check products

☒   Hand in products

❏   Discussion of academic skills

From *A Guidebook for Cooperative Learning* by Dee Dishon and Pat Wilson O'Leary. Holmes Beach, FL: Learning Publications, Inc., 1994.

Cooperative Learning
5-Step Lesson Plan Worksheet

Name _____   Class/Grade ___*4-8*___

Subject: ___*Science/Biology*___   # of Students _____

STEP 1.   Subject Matter Content

    A.   Learning Objective:

        Information/Skill to be learned: ___*Names and uses of bones of the human body*___

    B.   Group Goal: ___*Label major bones, understand functions, create new bone*___

    C.   Name of Strategy (if applicable): _____

    D.   Learning Experience(s) that precedes group work (lesson, video, etc.)

        ___*each group looking over skeleton model; video of skeletal system*___

    E.   Length of work time: ___*20*___ minutes

STEP 2.   Group Composition and Room Arrangement

    A.   Group Size: ___*4*___

    B.   Assignment to Groups (choose one):

        ❑ Random – – – – – – – Method: _____

        ☒ Teacher-Selected – – – Criteria: ___*boys/girls; interest in science*___

    C.   Duration of Groups: ___*Semester (Learning Buddies)*___

    D.   Room Arrangement: ___*Chairs around one end of table*___

From *A Guidebook for Cooperative Learning* by Dee Dishon and Pat Wilson O'Leary. Holmes Beach, FL: Learning Publications, Inc., 1994.

STEP 3.   **Positive Interdependence**

☒   A.   Materials   # Needed   Description

    ☒   Limited   *1*   *piece of paper: textbook*
                                 1   *set of markers*

    ❑   Jigsawed

☒   B.   One Product: *drawing of skeleton and explanation of new bone*

☒   C.   Common Goal: *each student works and agrees with labels and new bone*

☒   D.   Rotate Roles: *writer*   *drawer*   _____

❑   E.   Reward: _____   Criteria for receiving: _____

       Reason to use: _____

STEP 4.   **Individual Accountability**

☒   A.   Signatures (on front)
☒   B.   Random Check (explain method) *Winner's Hat for group reporter*
☒   C.   Individual performance (explain) *test on major bones*

STEP 5.   **Subject Matter Directions:** State in language your students will understand.

Your group will work cooperatively to:

1.   *Label all major bones of the human body. Reach consensus before anyone writes.*

2.   *Write down function of each bone labeled.*

3.   *Each take turn labeling and writing functions.*

4.   *All agree on new bone: name, location, and what its function would be.*

From *A Guidebook for Cooperative Learning* by Dee Dishon and Pat Wilson O'Leary. Holmes Beach, FL: Learning Publications, Inc., 1994.

5.   *Everyone be ready to report. Reporter will be randomly chosen. Indiv. quiz at end.*

6.   *Keep going until time is up. Then you will all sign to show agreement.*

    25 minutes work time

    Where to display for students: ☒ easel   ❑ chalkboard   ❑ screen

STEP 6.   Social Skill

Teacher-Used Observation Form:

    Contribute ideas

❑ One Group
☒ Multi-Group
❑ Classroom

STEP 7.   Process Social Skill (after work time)
(Choose one statement for students to complete)

❑ We did well on _____ by _____, _____, and _____.
               (social skill)   (specific behaviors)

❑ I liked the way I helped my group today by _____.

☒ In any group it is helpful to contribute ideas because _____.
                                                 (social skill)

STEP 8.   Process Subject Matter (after work time)

☒ Hear responses (all or some)

☒ See products (all or *some*)

❑ Students check products

☒ Hand in products

❑ Discussion of academic skills

From *A Guidebook for Cooperative Learning* by Dee Dishon and Pat Wilson O'Leary. Holmes Beach, FL: Learning Publications, Inc., 1994.

Cooperative Learning
5-Step Lesson Plan Worksheet

Name _____   Class/Grade ___*9-12*___

Subject ___*English*___   # of Students _____

STEP 1.   Subject Matter Content

    A.   Learning Objective:

        Information/Skill to be learned: ___*expand ideas for writing*___

    B.   Group Goal: ___*brainstorm & edit list of writing topics*___

    C.   Name of Strategy (if applicable): ___*Pairs of Pairs*___

    D.   Learning Experience(s) that precedes group work (lesson, video, etc.)

        ___*class discussion of journal writing*___

    E.   Length of work time: ___*3 & 7*___ minutes

STEP 2.   Group Composition and Room Arrangement

    A.   Group Size: ___*2's then 4's*___

    B.   Assignment to Groups (choose one):

        ☒ Random – – – – – – – Method: ___*"Winner's" Envelope*___

        ❑ Teacher-Selected – – – Criteria: _____

    C.   Duration of Groups: ___*this activity*___

    D.   Room Arrangement: ___*standing*___

From *A Guidebook for Cooperative Learning* by Dee Dishon and Pat Wilson O'Leary. Holmes Beach, FL: Learning Publications, Inc., 1994.

STEP 3. Positive Interdependence

☒ A.   Materials   # Needed   Description

        ☒ Limited   _1_   *clipboard*
                                      _1_   *piece of paper*

        ❑ Jigsawed   _____   _____

☒ B.   One Product: _*one completed, edited list*_____

❑ C.   Common Goal: _____

☒ D.   Rotate Roles: _*writer*_____   _____   _____

❑ E.   Reward: _____   Criteria for receiving: _____

           Reason to use: _____

STEP 4. Individual Accountability

☒ A.   Signatures (on front)

☒ B.   Random Check (explain method) _*Lettered heads — all groups*_____

❑ C.   Individual performance (explain) _____

STEP 5. Subject Matter Directions: State in language your students will understand.

Your group will work cooperatively to:

1. *Pairs-stand with 1 partner, brainstorm list of topics you could write about for journals; pass one paper back & forth so each of you write.*_____

2. *Pairs of Pairs-join your lists together; edit to avoid duplicates.*_____

3. *Agree on all final topics; take turns writing or marking on list. Sign to show agreement.*_____

From *A Guidebook for Cooperative Learning* by Dee Dishon and Pat Wilson O'Leary. Holmes Beach, FL: Learning Publications, Inc., 1994.

4. *Randomly chosen reporters will read 2 topics from list.*

5. *All lists will be hung on "Our Writing Topics" bulletin board.*

    3 & 7   minutes work time

Where to display for students: ☒ easel   ❑ chalkboard   ❑ screen

STEP 6.   Social Skill

Teacher-Used Observation Form:

   Respond to ideas respectfully   ❑ One Group
                                               ❑ Multi-Group
                                             ☒ Classroom

STEP 7.   Process Social Skill (after work time)
             (Choose one statement for students to complete)

❑ We did well on _____ by _____, _____, and _____.
                       (social skill)   (specific behaviors)

❑ I liked the way I helped my group today by _____.

☒ In any group it is helpful to *respond to ideas respectfully* because _____.
                                          (social skill)

STEP 8.   Process Subject Matter (after work time)

☒ Hear responses (all or *some*)

☒ See products (*all* or some)

❑ Students check products

❑ Hand in products

❑ Discussion of academic skills

From *A Guidebook for Cooperative Learning* by Dee Dishon and Pat Wilson O'Leary. Holmes Beach, FL: Learning Publications, Inc., 1994.

Choices for Processing Subject Matter

Choose *one* to complete. Choices range from lower to higher level thinking skills. Completed samples are given. See Chapter 3 for specific ways to use.

• Specific information we needed today was _____,

_____, and _____.

Sample: "Specific information we needed today was *punctuation, capitalization,* and *subject-verb agreement."*

• The resources we used were _____, _____, and

_____.

   Sample: "The resources we used were *a dictionary, atlas,* and *encyclopedia."*

• We learned that _____ means _____.
                   concept/skill   group's own words

Sample: "We learned that *tessellation* means *to form into patterns."*

• Another time or place to use this skill or knowledge of _____ is

_____.

Sample: "Another time or place to use this skill or knowledge of *long division* is *when planning servings of pizza."*

• The theory of _____ proved useful today because

_____.

Sample: "The theory of *least resistance* proved useful today because *we had to decide which materials gave way and which didn't break."*

From *A Guidebook for Cooperative Learning* by Dee Dishon and Pat Wilson O'Leary. Holmes Beach, FL: Learning Publications, Inc., 1994.

- To complete this project, we had to go through the steps of _____, _____, and _____.

    Sample: "To complete this project, we had to go through the steps of *listing, discussing,* and *crossing out.*"

- Today we used the skill of _____ rather than _____ because _____.

    Sample: "Today we used the skill of *editing* rather than *proofing* because *we needed to get out more ideas.*"

- We like our product because _____.

    Sample: "We like our product because *it has color and texture.*"

- Our product could be improved by _____ because _____.

    Sample: "Our product could be improved by *more information* because *it is sketchy.*"

- Skills we need to review are _____ because _____.

    Sample: "Skills we need to review are *guidewords* because *we looked at every page of the dictionary and didn't need to.*"

From *A Guidebook for Cooperative Learning* by Dee Dishon and Pat Wilson O'Leary. Holmes Beach, FL: Learning Publications, Inc., 1994.

Academic Tasks for Cooperative Groups:
A Starter List

Primary

- Match primary color cards with their names
- Edit writing samples (Daily Oral Language)
- Recognize whole numbers and fractions
- Match story titles with their main ideas
- Create new titles or endings for stories
- Build one structure from blocks
- Sequence events
- Check directions to and from given points
- Illustrate a story
- Match cloud shapes with predictable weather
- Cook using measuring instruments

Intermediate

- Create math story problems
- Write newsletter to parents
- Study spelling, vocabulary
- Identify, name constellations with research on myths
- Match states with capitals
- Proofread paragraphs for punctuation to match given rules
- Create and measure solid geometric shapes
- Read a thermometer in Celsius
- Identify continents, countries, states on maps
- Name and label primary and secondary colors
- Create science project, use scientific method

Junior High/Middle School

- Create math story problems
- Identify parts of speech
- Identify types of fabrics and decide how could be used

From *A Guidebook for Cooperative Learning* by Dee Dishon and Pat Wilson O'Leary. Holmes Beach, FL: Learning Publications, Inc., 1994.

- Check measurements to properly increase a recipe
- Match book categories to Dewey Decimal system
- Label bones of the body, parts of computer
- Edit writing selections
- Write newsletter for school
- Name components of a short story
- Know spelling and definitions of a list of homonyms
- Create science project, use scientific method

High School

- Compare and contrast elements from the Periodic Table
- Study vocabulary (for any content area)
- Identify machine parts and create safety rules
- Label literary forms of several readings
- Balance chemical equations
- Match name with function of body organs
- Analyze an IRS income tax form
- Identify reproductive parts of a flower
- Match symbols with advertised products and impact of symbol
- Check the computed costs of financing and running an automobile for one year
- Outline changes of power in Eastern Europe for ten year period

From *A Guidebook for Cooperative Learning* by Dee Dishon and Pat Wilson O'Leary. Holmes Beach, FL: Learning Publications, Inc., 1994.

Cooperative Strategies

Select or change the samples to fit the content you teach as well as the age and interest of your students. Notice that a variety of thinking skills are used within each strategy.

1. **Turn to Your Neighbor and** ... (say/write/draw)

    a. days of the week   e. metric terms
    b. nouns in room   f. symbols for minerals
    c. words that end with "e"   g. parts of an auto engine
    d. pairs of homonyms

    Students are randomly called upon to give/show group response.

2. **Think-Pair-Share**

    The teacher asks a question; students have time to think, the students talk in pairs, and finally some sharing takes place in the large group ("Winner's Envelope" for random, or volunteers tell what their partner said).

3. **Pairs of Pairs**

    Each person writes a list of responses to a question:

    a. what I'd like to study about _____   c. presents for Father's Day
    b. problems on the playground   d. topics for report on Abe Lincoln

    Two students are paired and combine their individual lists. They take turns writing: one paper and pencil. Then two pairs are paired up to combine two lists into one list: one paper and one pencil. Teacher collects ideas, one at a time from each group, until all ideas are written up.

4. **Advanced Pairs of Pairs**

    Students work in pairs to brainstorm as many ideas as they can on a topic for 3 minutes. One person writes: one paper and one pencil.

Possible topics:	classroom rules	consequences for unsatisfactory work
	events for field day	possible math problems that equal 21
	rewards for work	topics for creative writing

    Then two pairs are put together and they combine lists: one paper and one pencil.

From *A Guidebook for Cooperative Learning* by Dee Dishon and Pat Wilson O'Leary. Holmes Beach, FL: Learning Publications, Inc., 1994.

5. **Learning Buddies**

    Base groups of 3-4 students who meet frequently to:

    a. clarify, process information   d. review for test
    b. ask questions   e. practice
    c. translate information to practical situations

6. **Show & Tell / Bring & Brag** (for **All** ages!)

    Instead of the whole class listening to everyone's reports, current events, book reports, etc., each student shares in small groups (3-5). After a few minutes in which items are shared and discussed, students' names are randomly drawn ("Winner's Envelope"), and s/he tells about someone else's information.

7. **Dynamic Discussions**

    For discussions after an event that creates much interest and energy like:

    *   assembly   *   natural occurrence (earthquake/
    *   movie   first snowfall)
    *   field trip   *   guest in room
                                              *   important news event

    In group, write or draw **one** of the following (assigned by teacher) after group reaches consensus on:

    *   3 most important/exciting parts   *   something that surprised group
    *   new ending   *   what else could have happened
    *   group's favorite part   *   what might happen next (predict)

8. **Pairs and Practice Ideas**

    a. Pairs each work through the same set of problems or questions and then compare answers. Where they differ, they discuss why and attempt to find one solution. Or they compare answers with another pair and discuss which answer is correct and why. One worksheet is turned in to show agreed-upon answers.

    b. Each partner in the pair is responsible for every other problem, sentence, etc. When one is not working/writing, s/he watches and encourages. Then an answer sheet is used by the pair to check their work. The problems marked incorrect are then worked out together.

From *A Guidebook for Cooperative Learning* by Dee Dishon and Pat Wilson O'Leary. Holmes Beach, FL: Learning Publications, Inc., 1994.

9. **Jigsaw**

Using vocabulary or spelling, math facts or parts of an article, paragraph, story: the teacher cuts lists or information into equal parts, one for each group member. (NO ONE has the whole thing.) Students learn their own information and then teach to/share with their groupmates. No one may pass on his/her information: it can only be taught/shared by the person who has that part. Students can be held individually accountable by taking an individual oral or written test.

Expert Jigsaw

This works like jigsaw except each group member meets with students from several other groups who have the same material. They discuss, check information, decide how to teach/share. Then each goes back to his/her own group and teaches the information.

10. **Team Practice & Drill**

math facts
vocabulary/spelling words
definitions
chemical elements
} ON FLASHCARDS

Choose one type of practice. Make two envelopes labeled "Ours" and "Not Yet Ours." Put flashcards in appropriate envelope depending on whether or not group members know them. If each person has his/her own set of flashcards (students are not studying same words, facts, etc.), students put them in envelopes marked "Mine" and "Not Yet Mine."

11. **Numbered Heads Together**

Each person in the group is designated as a, b, c, d. Each group is designated as 1, 2, etc. Groups discuss a question for 2 minutes and prepare everyone to be the reporter. The teacher randomly picks a group number and a member letter out of the "Winner's Envelope." That person answers for the group. Then that letter and number go back into the envelope.

Sample questions: Where does the comma go?
                     How do you get 60%?
                     Why could 81 be the answer?
                     What are 3 possible answers?

From *A Guidebook for Cooperative Learning* by Dee Dishon and Pat Wilson O'Leary. Holmes Beach, FL: Learning Publications, Inc., 1994.

12. **Getting to Know Us**

Students interview one another in groups of 3 or 5 with prepared questions from the teacher like (choose 1 or 2):

- a favorite fall (winter/spring/summer) activity when I was younger
- a favorite place
- a fantasy weekend
- a career I would like

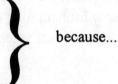 because...

The teacher RANDOMLY picks one person from each group to introduce another member of the group until all have been introduced to the class. Each person must be prepared because they will NOT be able to choose who they are to introduce.

13. **Groups and Homework** (Homework can require either "right answers" or open-ended responses.)

Students sit in Check-In groups which review homework daily. The group encourages individuals to complete homework assignments and bring in on time. Patterns may be seen by filling in a grid each day in the group folder.

Group members compare answers on homework. The team comes to a consensus on what each answer should be (ALL agree). The group submits to the teacher ONE answer sheet with consensus answers on it which all group members sign, indicating understanding and agreement. All individual homework sheets are stapled to the back of the group answer sheet.

(Adapted from, and with thanks to, work by Liana Graves, Ted Graves, Spencer Kagan, Frank Lyman.)

From *A Guidebook for Cooperative Learning* by Dee Dishon and Pat Wilson O'Leary. Holmes Beach, FL: Learning Publications, Inc., 1994.

Samples of Team Building Activities

These activities help students get to know team members. (See Chapter 3 for explanation.)

WHIPS: Each student in the group gives a response with no comments by others until everyone has had a turn. Topics can include: a favorite _____ (and why) — place; book; sport; musician; TV show; video; pet; movie. Content related favorites may include: planet; state; flower; continent; politician; author; play; short story; scientist; explorer; etc.

Use a variety of strategies to help students decide who will go first. Ideas include: person whose birthday is closest to today or in this month; person with _____ eyes, _____ shirt/blouse, _____ shoes, most pets, fewest brothers and sisters, lives furthest/closest to school, etc.

M & M Turn-Taking Strategy — Students pass around M & M's after being told to "Take as many as you need for the next activity." Be sure NOT to tell what the activity is. Then students respond to whip statement as many times as they have M & M's (each response must be different). To keep this activity fresh, ask students next time to respond as many times as they have red M & M's (or any other color picked by teacher).

"WHAT'S IN A NAME?": Students do pair of pairs activity each telling his/her partner about who s/he was named for, history of the name; nickname preferred; name I'd rather have; etc. After a set time (1 or 2 minutes), each partner introduces her/his partner to a new pair. Then the teacher randomly calls on students and tells them whose name they will tell the class about (only do a few unless interest is high and you have the time to do more.)

"GROUP NAME": Each group decides on a name that shows commonality. Be sure to note that each name is to be POSITIVE. You may want to check each group's name before it is written up for the class to see.

It is helpful to create group folders, especially when a group is to stay together for any length of time and they are doing work together. Use a manila folder or a construction paper folder to hold all group materials, especially unfinished work, papers to be referred to later, observation forms, etc. When a new group begins, a new folder is made. The folder may be decorated with the group name, group logo or picture to illustrate name. Students may also put in information from whips, "Cooperation is..." and other team building activities.

"COOPERATION IS..." — Group uses magazines to find pictures of cooperation. Pictures are arranged into a collage or arrangement and can include a paragraph telling what about the picture(s) indicates cooperation.

After sharing some/all with the class (use randomly chosen reporters), put finished products into a class book, which can be checked out of the classroom library or is available in the Nostalgia Corner/Our Classroom Archives.

From *A Guidebook for Cooperative Learning* by Dee Dishon and Pat Wilson O'Leary. Holmes Beach, FL: Learning Publications, Inc., 1994.

Primary Adaption

Students find several pictures, check for agreement, and then glue onto a piece of colored construction paper. Aide/helper can help them write why these show cooperation.

Elementary/Junior High Adaption

Each group finds several pictures that show cooperation and agrees on one picture that is best example of cooperation. Then they write a rough draft explaining what this has to do with cooperation. After proofreading and editing, paragraph is copied over (each student does a part) and glued beneath the picture. After sharing some/all with the class (use randomly chosen reporters), put finished products up on the bulletin board. Have students compare/contrast, notice similarities/differences with what they found, etc.

Responses go into group folder. Put into the Our Classroom Archives in a class book after they have been up for 2-3 weeks.

High School Adaption

Follow directions above, adding quotations from famous people, samples from students' own lives, application in current world situation, etc.

"ME IN A SHOWBOX": — Students put several items in a shoebox that shows how they are a special person. Students decorate the outside of the box with words, pictures, drawings that tell about their own personality, interests, favorites, people s/he loves, etc. In groups, students pass around "Me Boxes" WITHOUT talking. They take their time, examine each box carefully, being sure to study the inside and outside. After each group member has studied each box, students take turns going around the circle and sharing onething they learned about each of the other students in the group. In a large circle of the whole class, students take turns telling one new thing s/he learned about a member of their group (May be done by everyone or those whose names are drawn from the "Winner's Envelope.")

Primary Adaption

One favorite object that fits into box. On outside draw or paste pictures of favorite food, clothes, pets, family members, etc.

Elementary/Junior High/High School Adaption:

Three favorite objects. If they don't fit into the box, students may draw. Decorate outside of box with words, pictures, drawings that tell about individual's personality, interests, favorites, family members, friends, etc.

From *A Guidebook for Cooperative Learning* by Dee Dishon and Pat Wilson O'Leary. Holmes Beach, FL: Learning Publications, Inc., 1994.

Resources

References in this Guidebook

Albert, Linda. *A Teacher's Guide to Cooperative Discipline.* Circle Pines, MN: American Guidance Service, 1989.

Costa, Art. *The School As A Home For The Mind.* Palatine, Illinois: Skylight Publishing, 1991.

Dishon, Dee & Pat Wilson O'Leary. *Cooperation Unlimited INK,* newsletter for teachers and administrators. P.O. Box 68, Portage, MI 49002, (616) 327-2199, 1986 to present.

Faber, Adele & Elaine Mazlish. *How To Talk So Kids Will Listen & Listen So Kids Will Talk.* New York, NY: Rawson, Wade Publishers, 1980.

Kohn, Alfie. *No Contest: The Case Against Competition.* Boston, MA: Houghton Mifflin Co., 1992.

Moorman, Chick & Dee Dishon. *Our Classroom: We Can Learn Together.* Cooperation Unlimited, P.O. Box 68, Portage, MI 49081, (616) 327- 2199.

Nelsen, Jane. *Positive Discipline.* New York: Ballantine Books, 1987.

Slavin, Robert. *Using Student Team Learning.* 3rd. Edition, Baltimore, MD: Johns Hopkins University, 1986.

Readings for General Information

Brandt, Ronald. Readings from Educational Leadership. *Cooperative Learning and the Collaborative School.* Alexandria, VA: Association for Supervision and Curriculum Development, 1250 N. Pitt Street, Alexandria, VA 22314, 1991.

Clarke, Judy. *Together We Learn.* Scarborough, Ontario: Prentice-Hall Canada Inc., 1990.

Davidson, Neil. *Cooperative Learning in Mathematics.* Addison-Wesley Innovative Division, 1990.

Davidson, Neil & Toni Worsham. *Enhancing Thinking Through Cooperative Learning.* New York, NY: Teachers College Press, Columbia University, 1992.

Glasser, William. *The Quality School.* New York, NY: HarperCollins Publishing Inc., 2nd ed., 1992.

Graves, Drs. Nancy & Ted. *Getting There Together.* Cooperative College of California, 136 Liberty Street, Santa Cruz, CA 95060, 1988.

Graves, Liana and Ted Graves, editors. *Cooperative Learning: The Magazine for Cooperation in Education.* P.O. Box 1582, Santa Cruz, CA 95061-1582.

Johnson, David W. & Roger T. Johnson. *Learning Together and Alone: Cooperation, Competition and Individualization.* Needham Heights, MA: Allyn & Bacon, 1991.

Kagan, Spencer. *Cooperative Learning.* Kagan's Cooperative Learning Company, 27128 Paseo Espada, Suite 602, San Juan Capistrano, CA 92675, 1992.

Roy, Pat. *Cooperative Learning: Students Learning Together.* Patricia Roy Company, 3600 N. Spruce Street, Wilmington, DE 19802, 1990.

Sharan, Yael & Shlomo Sharan. *Expanding Cooperative Learning Through Group Investigation.* New York, NY: Teachers College Press, Columbia University, 1992.

Organizations

The International Association for the Study of Cooperation in Education (IASCE)
P.O. Box 1582
Santa Cruz, CA 95061-1582 U.S.A.
Phone: (408) 426-7926; Fax: (408) 426-3360.

The Cooperative Learning Network
Sponsored by the Association for Supervision and Curriculum Development (ASCD)
Administrative Center
2000 N.E. E. 46th Street
Kansas City, MO 64116.
Phone: (816) 453-5050.

Cooperative Games

Animal Town Game Company
P.O. Box 485
Healdsburg, CA 95448.

Family Pastimes
RR#4
Perth, Ontario, CANADA K7H 3C6

From *A Guidebook for Cooperative Learning* by Dee Dishon and Pat Wilson O'Leary. Holmes Beach, FL: Learning Publications, Inc., 1994.